1936

ALISON'S HOUSE

ALISON'S HOUSE

A Play in Three Acts

BY

SUSAN GLASPELL

SAMUEL FRENCH

Thos. R. Edwards   Managing Director

NEW YORK   LOS ANGELES

SAMUEL FRENCH Ltd.   LONDON

1930

First Printing December 1930
Second Printing March 1931
Third Printing May 1931
Fourth Printing May 1931
Fifth Printing May 1931
Sixth Printing November 1931

MANUFACTURED IN THE UNITED STATES OF AMERICA
BY THE VAIL-BALLOU PRESS, INC., BINGHAMTON, N. Y.

"ALISON'S HOUSE" produced by the Civic Repertory Theatre, New York City, on December 1, 1930, under the direction of Eva Le Gallienne. Costumes and scenery designed by Aline Bernstein. The cast was as follows:

ANN LESLIE	*secretary*	.... *Florida Friebus*
JENNIE	*(maid?)*	.... *Leona Roberts*
RICHARD KNOWLES	*reporter*	.... *Robert Ross*
TED STANHOPE	*son*	.... *Herbert Shapiro*
LOUISE	*daughter-in-law*	.... *Josephine Hutchinson*
THE FATHER	*dad*	.... *Walter Beck*
EBEN	*son (twin's husband)*	.... *Donald Cameron*
ELSA	*daughter*	.... *Eva Le Gallienne*
MISS AGATHA	*sister*	.... *Alma Kruger*
HODGES	*(prospective ...)*	.... *Howard da Silva*
MRS. HODGES	*(... buyers)*	.... *Mary Ward*

Period—December 31, 1899

ACT I

The library of the old Stanhope homestead in Iowa,
on the Mississippi.

ACT II

The same as Act I.

ACT III

Alison's room.

11181

ACT ONE

ACT ONE

Scene: The library of the old Stanhope homestead in Iowa, on the Mississippi, where MISS AGATHA STANHOPE *still lives. There is a river village near-by, and the small city where the other* STANHOPES *now live is about ten miles up the river.*

It is the room of people who have lived in comfortable circumstances and signifies a family of traditions and cultivation.

Left, just rear of center, a door into the hall. In the rear corner, left, a stone fireplace. In the rear wall a bay-window, the windows coming down to a low seat, and curtained with old plum-colored velvet. Right of this are books, which are continued into an alcove. There is an easy chair near the bay-window, by it a foot-stool and a low table; front, right, a long table. At the left, front of door, a desk. The room is carpeted, a tone deeper than the curtains. On the walls are portraits of an older generation.

The time is eleven in the morning of the last day of the nineteenth century, December 31, 1899. But the furnishings of the library are of a period earlier than this.

As the curtain rises ANN *is seated before her Oliver typewriter, near the alcove, behind the long table. She is fair, sensitive looking. She wears a shirt waist and blue skirt, in the manner of 1900. She is about twenty-three, and has gentle manners. She reaches down and takes an-*

3

other old paper from a small horse-hair trunk beside her.
Makes a typewritten note.

[*Enter* JENNIE.

JENNIE (*speaking to some one behind her*)

You had better come in here. Everything is so upset
—with the moving. Oh, here is Miss Ann. He says he's
a reporter, Miss. I don't know anything about it.

[*Enter* KNOWLES, *a young man.* JENNIE *goes out.*

ANN

You wished to see Mr. Stanhope?

KNOWLES

Well—yes, some of the family. But most of all, the
house.

ANN

The house is being broken up.

KNOWLES

I want to see it before it's broken up. Especially the
room that was used by Miss Alison Stanhope.

ANN

I think no one goes in that room, except the family.

KNOWLES

You are not—of the family?

ANN

Oh, no. I am Mr. Stanhope's secretary.

KNOWLES (*going a little nearer*)

Those papers you're working with—are they by any
chance the papers of Miss Alison Stanhope?

ANN

They are not.

KNOWLES (*with his very nice smile*)

And it's none of my business what they are. I'm from the Chicago Record Herald. Down to get a little story about the house, because it is being broken up.

ANN (*with a smile*)

Isn't there anything going on in Chicago?

KNOWLES

Perhaps not as much as went on in this house.

ANN

I'm surprised a metropolitan paper should be interested in the fact Miss Agatha Stanhope is moving up to town to live with her brother.

KNOWLES

It isn't Miss Agatha. It's Miss Alison.

ANN

But aren't you a little late? Miss Alison has been dead eighteen years.

KNOWLES

She isn't dead. Anything about her is alive. She belongs to the world. But the family doesn't seem to know that.

ANN

They published her poems.

KNOWLES

But anything about where—how—they were written.
The desk she sat at. The window she looked from. Is
there a bird singing in that tree now? Well, no, probably not, the last day of December. But looking
through the dead branches, to meadows sloping to the
Mississippi, as she looked.

ANN

You cared for the poems.

KNOWLES

I'll never forget the day I got them—at the bookshop
on the Midway, and walked down through Jackson
Park, and saw the lake—because she had seen the
river. I write a little poetry myself.

ANN

I wish I could. But I can't write it. That's why I'm so
grateful to Alison.

KNOWLES

I know. Do you read the Record Herald?

ANN

Usually.

KNOWLES

Did you see it last Wednesday?

ANN

I don't remember.

KNOWLES

Do you remember a poem—no, verses—Michigan
Avenue?

ANN

I'm afraid I didn't see that.

KNOWLES (*grinning*)

Well, I did.

ANN

You get your poems printed?

KNOWLES

I'm no Alison, but—

ANN

I suppose you haven't it with you?

KNOWLES

Well, since you mention it, I don't seem to remember taking it out of my vest pocket.

ANN

I'd love to see it.

KNOWLES

You would? Oh, well, I don't mind. (*Taking a clipping from his pocket, he hands it to her.*) Don't *expect* anything.

ANN (*who is reading*)

Oh, I think that's nice.

KNOWLES (*eagerly looking over her shoulder*)

Which part?

ANN

The lake. "Through all the years you waited for your city—"

KNOWLES

Just a fancy. I like best— "Lights snuffed in fog as—"
[TED *comes in, whistling "A hot time in the old town tonight."*

ANN

Ted! Here is a poem about— (*To* KNOWLES.) Oh, here is a member of the family, Mr. Edward Stanhope. This gentleman—

KNOWLES

Knowles.

ANN

Mr. Knowles is a reporter. He's from the Record Herald.

TED

Honest?

KNOWLES (*laughing*)

Honest.

ANN

He wants to see the house.

TED

Should have come sooner. Everything's topsy-turvy. Anyway—why?

KNOWLES

Because Alison Stanhope lived and died here.

TED

I see. Well, they haven't started on Alison's room yet. Aunt Agatha won't let them.

KNOWLES

Won't you let me see it? It isn't just the story. It's—a feeling about it. (*To* ANN.) You know. And since it's going to be broken up, and won't be any more, why not some one who has a feeling about it to—to hold it in memory, you might say.

TED (*uncertainly*)

Well, I dunno.

ANN

I've been in there. Mr. Stanhope took me when I got here this morning. He said he wanted me to be there— before it ceased. It's just the same. It's as if she might come in the door.

KNOWLES

We understand. We three. Why trouble the older folks about it? This is the last day of the nineteenth century.

TED

Well, there's no lie, but—

KNOWLES

I can't tell you how I'd appreciate it. How much it would mean to me.

TED (*at the door, looking into the hall*)

They're all in the dining-room, counting dishes.

KNOWLES

Fine!

TED

But if Louise finds out.

KNOWLES

She won't. We'll see to it.

TED (*attracted by the idea of stealing a march*)

S—h.

[*Goes out, softly, followed by* KNOWLES. ANN *returns to the poem she had not finished.*

[*Enter* LOUISE.

LOUISE (*sharply*)

What is this story of Jennie's—about a reporter?

ANN

There was a reporter.

LOUISE

Did you talk to him?

ANN

Not much.

LOUISE

Where is he?

ANN

He went out just now.

LOUISE

Where?

ANN

Why, just out.

LOUISE

You refuse to talk to me—about a family matter?

ANN (*examining a paper from the trunk*)

There is so much for me to do.

LOUISE

Well—really. We'll see about this! (*Goes to the door.*)
Father! Father Stanhope!

ANN

Oh—please! Surely that isn't necessary, when he's so
busy—troubled.

LOUISE

So am I busy—troubled. Yes, Father. Just a moment,
please.
[*Enter* STANHOPE. *He has the look of a man who has
made a place for himself, who is acquainted with re-
sponsibilities. He is vigorous for a man of sixty-three,
though troubled at the moment. One soon feels he has
a feeling for others that makes him tolerant, though
firm.*

STANHOPE (*good humoredly*)

What's the trouble now?

LOUISE

Father, I think you ought to know there's a reporter
in the house. Ann knows about it, and won't tell.

STANHOPE

Yes? Well, when you've seen as many reporters as I
have you'll know they don't usually shoot, or even
bite. He probably came down about the Mahoney case.

LOUISE (*to* ANN)

Where was he from?

ANN

Chicago.

LOUISE

Chicago! You see? "The Mahoney case"!

STANHOPE

What did he want, Ann?

ANN

To see the house.

LOUISE

Why? Why should he see the house?

ANN

Because Alison lived here.

LOUISE

I knew that!

STANHOPE

Well, and what of it? My dear, you can't have a dis-
tinguished person in the family without running into
a little public interest.
[*He takes one of the papers from the trunk.*

LOUISE

Father! Please let's try to do this without—stirring
things up. Just because we're breaking up the house
do we have to revive the stories about Alison?

STANHOPE

To what stories about my sister do you refer?

LOUISE

Now please don't be vexed with me. You know as well
as I do—the whole story they've harped on so long—

that she was different—a rebel—goodness, I don't know what they do mean.

STANHOPE

I think the worst they can say about my dear sister is that she was a great soul, and a poet. It isn't going to hurt my feelings to have it said again.

LOUISE

But you know how they talk—it makes the whole family seem—different. And after Elsa— (*At this change.*) Oh, forgive me, but you must know how the town does talk about Elsa. You can't run away with a married man—live with a man who has a wife and children and not be talked about.

ANN

In making the memoranda of these old contracts am I to—
[STANHOPE *moves to her.*

LOUISE

And they do link it up with something queer about Alison.

STANHOPE (*checking anger, and speaking easily*)

That would be most unjust to Alison. She never lived with a man who had a wife and children.

LOUISE (*knowing she shouldn't say it*)

She wanted to, didn't she?

STANHOPE (*again checking anger, speaking humorously*)

Oh we want to do lots of things we don't do. I might

want to ask my daughter-in-law to keep still. In fact, I think I shall.

LOUISE (*rather angry, and made the more persistent by it*)

Where did he go—this reporter?

ANN

Why they went out—just a moment ago.

LOUISE

They? Who's with him?

ANN

He's with Ted.

LOUISE

Ted! He's already told him enough to fill a page! Where did they go?

STANHOPE (*as* ANN *peers at a paper*)

Well, where did they go, Ann—the roof—the cellar?

ANN

He wanted to see the Alison room.

LOUISE

And you dared—and Ted dared— Oh what *management*.

[*She moves to the door, but* STANHOPE *follows*.

STANHOPE

No. Not up there. No disturbance in Alison's room. It is to keep its—serenity, the one day it has left.

LOUISE

Serenity! With reporters prowling around?

ANN

He writes poetry himself.

LOUISE

How absurd!

ANN

No, it was quite good.

LOUISE

The trouble is, Father, the family has too many—on the outskirts, who like to snatch a little of the sensationalism. I'm amazed you can't see my point. Just now, after Elsa—

STANHOPE

I have told you before I did not wish to discuss my daughter with you.

LOUISE

But you act as if I had nothing to do with it. Your daughter is my husband's sister—I'm sorry to say. My children are Stanhopes. I don't want them taunted.

STANHOPE

Have they been taunted? They're rather young for that.

LOUISE

They will be.

STANHOPE

Well, sufficient unto the day is the taunting thereof.

LOUISE

But if we stir it all up again—

STANHOPE

The family china and silver seem more important at the moment than the family disgraces. I hadn't thought you need come down here, Louise, but you were anxious to get your Aunt Agatha moved with the least friction. Now why not a little management in the dining-room? Poor Agatha's all upset.

LOUISE (*starting to go, but turning*)

It isn't good for Eben, either!

STANHOPE (*occupied with a paper*)

The dining-room?

LOUISE

Oh, Father, why won't you be serious with me?

STANHOPE

Because you make me feel too serious, perhaps.

LOUISE

Eben isn't any too well grounded.

STANHOPE

Oh Eben has a very good hold on the law.

LOUISE

I mean the law of *life*.

STANHOPE

Oh. Law of life.

LOUISE

He has that same thing. He could just—shake everything loose. I'm sorry to talk before outsiders.

STANHOPE

I don't regard Ann an outsider. It was you came where
she was working, not Ann who intruded. Now Ann,
take these notes, please.

LOUISE

I think a family should stand together.

STANHOPE

That's right. Stand by your Aunt Agatha.

LOUISE (*murmuring as she goes out*)

What can I *do?*

STANHOPE (*sitting down by* ANN, *she with her pad for
dictation*)

Sometimes I wish I weren't the head of a family.
Sometimes I wish there weren't any family. (ANN *had
begun to take this, tears off the page.*) Quite so. Some
things we never put down. Even Alison didn't put it
all down. (*Listening to footsteps in the hall.*) Ted!
(TED *comes to the door.*) Come in here. Both of you.
[KNOWLES *follows* TED *into the room.*

TED

This is Mr. Knowles, Father.

STANHOPE (*curtly*)

How do you do?

KNOWLES

How do you do, sir.

STANHOPE (*to* TED)

What have you been doing?

TED

Just walking around.

STANHOPE

Where?

TED

Round the house.

STANHOPE

What room of the house?

KNOWLES

My fault, sir. I wanted to see Miss Alison's room.

STANHOPE

You did, did you? A great many people have wanted to see it, and haven't.

KNOWLES (*to* TED)

I want to thank you for letting me see it.

STANHOPE

He had no business to let you see it!

KNOWLES

Nevertheless I shall remember it always.

STANHOPE (*momentarily touched by the sincerity of his tone*)

And now you're going to write a lurid story about it.

KNOWLES

Not lurid. (*With a smile.*) That wouldn't be the way
to handle this story. But that room belongs to the
world, don't you think so? Alison Stanhope's room—
holds something.

[AGATHA STANHOPE *has appeared in the doorway; she
retains the manner of strength, though obviously
feeble. She is carrying a china tea-pot, and a sugar
bowl. She is arrested by* KNOWLES' *last words.*

AGATHA

What does it hold? (*Fearful of dropping the tea-pot
she holds it against her.*) What does it hold?

STANHOPE

Never mind, Agatha.
[*He tries to take the pieces she carries, but she does
not give them to him.*

AGATHA

What is he here for?

STANHOPE

It's all right, Agatha.
[*He guides her to the big chair, would help her seat
herself.*

AGATHA

What does he know about it?

STANHOPE

Nothing. Nothing at all.
[*Enter* JENNIE, *carrying a large basket filled with
straw, on the top of which is another piece of the tea
set.*

JENNIE

I think this will be all right, Miss Agatha.

[*She puts it down, goes out.* AGATHA *still looking at the reporter. With* STANHOPE's *help she is seated, as if not knowing it has happened.*

STANHOPE (*pulling up the low table for the tea things*)

You needn't do these things yourself.

AGATHA

What does it hold? It holds nothing, I tell you—nothing. (*Making as if to rise.*) Did you take something?

KNOWLES

Oh, no. Indeed I did not.

AGATHA (*to* STANHOPE)

He's looking for something.

STANHOPE

No, Agatha. Just some one here with Ted. (*Low, to* TED.) You haven't done so well, you see.

AGATHA

I won't have people looking through Alison's room. I've guarded it for eighteen years. (*Changing, cunning.*) All right, look. Look again. See what you find.

STANHOPE

We'll say good day now, young man.

KNOWLES

One question, please. Sorry. I was told to ask it. Have all the poems of Alison Stanhope been published?

AGATHA (*who had begun taking out the straw for packing*)

What's that? What does he mean?

STANHOPE (*soothing her*)

Never mind. I will answer your question, though I've answered it many times before. All the poems of Alison Stanhope have been published.

AGATHA

Now. You see? He answered you, didn't he?

KNOWLES

In going through the house—going through old papers—did you—

STANHOPE

It was one question you were to ask.

KNOWLES

Please, just this. It is a matter of public concern, you know. Did you find any papers—

AGATHA

What papers? What papers is he talking about?

STANHOPE

My sister is not equal to this. No, we found nothing that brings any new light to bear on the life of Alison Stanhope. Everything had been gone through long before.

AGATHA

Everything had been gone through long before.

KNOWLES

Thank you, sir. (*To* AGATHA.) Sorry to have disturbed you.

AGATHA (*sharply*)

You didn't disturb me.

KNOWLES (*to* ANN, *with a smile*)

Goodbye.

ANN (*holding it out to him*)

I like the poem.

KNOWLES

Would you like to keep it?

ANN

Thank you.
[KNOWLES *goes out, followed by* TED.

AGATHA

Where did he come from? What does he want?

STANHOPE

It's nothing—nothing at all. (*To himself.*) We're lucky to get off this easy.

AGATHA

That's why I didn't want to move. Stirring it all up! I wish they'd let Alison alone.

STANHOPE

They will, dear—in time.

AGATHA

Why can't they let her rest in peace?

STANHOPE

They will—soon. Though it wasn't in peace Alison rested.

AGATHA

What do you mean? I knew her better than you did.

STANHOPE

No you didn't, Agatha. But never mind. Now you don't have to pack these things yourself.

AGATHA

Mother's tea set? I'll pack it myself, and take it with me myself.

ANN

Perhaps I could help you, Miss Agatha. (*To* STANHOPE.) Have I time?

STANHOPE (*nodding*)

We don't make much headway, anywhere. (*He sits at the table, discouraged.*) It's harder than I thought.

AGATHA

I wouldn't have believed it, John. I just wouldn't have believed that you—our brother John—would break up the old place, turning me out of home.

STANHOPE

That's because I want to turn you into my own home. You have to take care of me now, Agatha.

AGATHA

Elsa went away and left you.

STANHOPE (*hurt, but again speaking brightly*)

So you have to step into the breach, as usual.

AGATHA

I looked after Alison—so long. Then looked after what Alison left. Now you're turning her out of home.

STANHOPE

Don't say that. She wouldn't say it. Alison was at home in the universe.

AGATHA

Elsa shouldn't have gone away and left her father.

STANHOPE

No.

AGATHA

Alison wouldn't have.

STANHOPE

No, Alison didn't do it—that way. But we differ. We're all different.

AGATHA

Alison stayed.

STANHOPE

Yes.
[ANN *has been packing the tea set.*

AGATHA (*looking down at it*)

No—no, those are too near together.

ANN (*taking one out*)

Then I'll fix it—this way.
[TED *returns.*

TED

Nice fellow.

STANHOPE (*at the table, looking through papers*)

You exceeded your authority, young man.

TED

We can't keep Alison in a prison.

AGATHA

Who kept Alison in a prison? What do you mean—a prison? She was where she wanted to be, wasn't she?

TED

She doesn't belong to just us. She belongs to the world.

STANHOPE

Oh, come Ted. We've heard that times enough, and acted on it.

AGATHA

I say she does not belong to the world! I say she belongs to us. And I'll keep her from the world—I'll keep the world from getting her—if it kills me—and kills you all!

TED (*at first standing there, astonished by the outburst*)

Well, I hope it doesn't.

[*Sits at the desk, taking paper and pen.*

STANHOPE (*going over to* TED)

Now that is enough. One more word to agitate her, and you'll answer to me. (*Low.*) I told you what the doctor said. (*As* ANN *rises, after packing the tea*

set.) Well, that's in good shape, isn't it, Agatha?
Now you finish up here, Ann, and Ted will help you
list the books.

TED

Soon's I finish this letter. He won't give me the grade
unless I tell him.

AGATHA

Who are you writing to?

TED

My English prof.

AGATHA

What about?

TED

Alison.

STANHOPE

Keep quiet or leave the room!

TED

Gee, Father, there's no other room to go to. They're
all torn up.

AGATHA

What's he telling him?

STANHOPE

Nothing. He's just acting important. Now Agatha—
Michael is here with the carriage. There's no reason
for your sitting in this confusion. I'm going to have
him drive you to the village for the noon train. That
will get you to town in twenty minutes. Louise can go

with you; or Ann, if you prefer. There you'll be comfortable, and can rest.

AGATHA

Me leave this house—while it is still this house? I shall be the last to step from the door.

STANHOPE

Oh, Agatha. You make it so hard for yourself, and for us all.

AGATHA

Leave things for every one else to pry into—looking —prying.

TED

What kind of a pen did Alison use, and where is the pen?

STANHOPE

Be still!

TED

Well, gee, she's my aunt, isn't she, and you want me to be flunked in English?

AGATHA (*low, gloatingly*)

He doesn't know what kind of a pen she used—and I won't tell.

STANHOPE

No; why should you?
[*He goes over to the books. Is looking at titles. For a moment* AGATHA *watches* TED. *She gets an idea, shrinks*

*from it; it is terrible to her, but it grows, she faces it,
and for a time she is aware of nothing else, does not
move.*

STANHOPE (*as* ANN *puts aside papers*)

You are through there now?

ANN

I think so.

STANHOPE

Suppose we start on the books. We don't have to do it
very minutely, but must have something of a cata-
logue, as they go to different people. (ANN *gets ready
for this.* STANHOPE *glances at his sister, but a little
bent now, turned from him, he does not see her eyes,
their horror, and purpose. Low.*) Poetry. The Mer-
maid series, twelve volumes.

[TED *tears off his sheet of paper, crumples it, kicks the
leg of the desk, rubs his head.*

TED (*muttering*)

What's anybody *go* to college for? Gee! (*Takes another sheet, considers.*) Gee, whiz!

STANHOPE

Chaucer. (*Taking one out.*) These are old. (*Reads a
little.*) Alison read it aloud—beautifully. Her voice—
(*Stands as if listening. Abruptly breaks from this.*)
Two volumes. (*Puts the book back.* AGATHA *begins to
unpack the tea set. Looks around to see that her
brother is not watching her. Works carefully, to make
no noise. Puts the pieces at the side of her chair, where
the others will not see. Presses the straw back in the*

basket.) Spencer. The Faery Queen. (*Waits for her to write*.) Greene, Marlowe, Jonson.

ANN

All one volume?

STANHOPE

Yes.

TED

Oh—*rats*.
[*Rubs his head*.

STANHOPE

Shakespeare, five volumes. (*Takes out the next book, examines it*.) This is a nice old edition of Milton. See? (*Showing it to* ANN.) Alison was fond of this book.

ANN

Funny old pictures, aren't they?
[AGATHA *gets her hands under the basket, which is on the low table. With difficulty rises, and takes it from the room*.

STANHOPE

But we must get on with it. (*Hearing his sister as she is leaving the room*.) Agatha? (*As she does not pause*.) Well, her last day here. Now we come to Robert Burns —good Bobbie.

ANN

One volume?

STANHOPE

Yes. And Browning—Robert, four volumes; Mrs. Browning—

[*Enter* LOUISE.

LOUISE

This is the table to be sent to Cousin Marion, isn't it? [*Her hand on the low table from which* AGATHA *has taken the basket.*

STANHOPE

Do we need to tear up this room just now?

LOUISE

The man is here—and if we are to finish by day after tomorrow.

TED

Did Alison sleep well?

STANHOPE

Really, Ted, sometimes I think you haven't good sense.

TED

I've got sense enough to know how I can make this grade. You ought to hear *him*. He takes me out for dinner—fills me up on wine—

LOUISE

Who?

TED

Styles—English prof.

LOUISE

Your teachers at Harvard take you out and give you wine?

TED

Only Styles. Ever since he heard I was her nephew.
Nearly dropped dead first time he asked me. But it
always ends telling me I got no soul—insensitive family—unworthy. He's crazy. Got to get this grade
though.

LOUISE

Father, you surely won't permit Ted to write a stranger—telling things—stirring it all up.

STANHOPE

Take the table out for Louise, Ted.

LOUISE

What is the tea set doing on the floor? Not a very safe
place for valuable old china.
[*She picks up the tea-pot and puts it on the big table,
is getting the other pieces.*

STANHOPE (*to* ANN)

Why I thought you packed that tea set.

ANN

I did.

STANHOPE

And she unpacked it?

LOUISE

And left it on the floor.

ANN

But she was so anxious about it.

STANHOPE

I'm afraid. Afraid for Agatha.

TED

Now about what Alison ate.

LOUISE

Seems to me it's Ted whose mind is failing.

STANHOPE

We're not in the mood for this nonsense.

TED

It's no nonsense to me—after flunking history. What did she eat, Father? Did she like sweets?

LOUISE

Ted might as well be in town.

TED

Meat. How about meat?

STANHOPE (*going back to the books*)

No one is paying any attention to you. (*Firmly.*) Tennyson.

TED

Then how am I to get through college?

LOUISE (*who is dusting the small table*)

I always said Ted should be sent to a western school. At least the professors don't intoxicate the students.

TED

He never got me full but once. Then he was trying to find out about her love affair.

STANHOPE (*angrily*)

Shelley. Four volumes.

LOUISE

You see? All this prying. Why it's as if the family weren't anything *else*. Why not tell him your grandfather was governor of the state and that your uncle is in Congress?

TED

He says the rest of the family is of interest only because it's so vacuous. Vacuous, is that the word? But about the food, Father. I got to get this letter off before he reads what I handed in. Meat. Sweets. Fruit. (*Writes.*) Lots of fruit.

STANHOPE

And Keats.
[*He stands looking through the Keats.*
[*A door closes outside.*

EBEN (*off*)

How are you, Jennie?

STANHOPE

Why that's Eben.

EBEN (*off*)

Oh but you'll like it in town. Lots more going on. You can go to church.

JENNIE (*off, in a dismal voice*)

I'm out of the habit.
[EBEN *enters. He is self-assured in manner, though*

soon one feels the inner uncertainties, hesitations, and the inner beauty.

EBEN

How are you, Father? Working hard, Louise?

LOUISE

Certainly.

EBEN

Hello, Ann. (*To* TED *who stares moodily.*) Well, I see you're energetically on the job.

TED (*solemnly*)

I am doing my best.

EBEN

Who could do more?

TED (*gloomily*)

Who?

LOUISE

I thought you weren't coming down till the office closed.

EBEN

I closed it. Nobody wants to do anything—last day of the year—last day of the century. Nobody's busy but Cousin Marion. She telephoned three times. Thinks her club women might take the house for a museum.

STANHOPE

She's thought that for two years. They haven't the money.

EBEN

She says they could get a little, and pay gradually—
give a kermiss or something.

STANHOPE

We'll close with Hodges, who doesn't have to give a
kermiss.

EBEN

Her idea would hold the place together.

STANHOPE

Hold it together for the public. Agatha would never
submit to it.

EBEN

How is she?

STANHOPE

Not well. Over excited, which is just what the doctor
warned against. I want to tell you, all of you—are
you listening, Ted?—nothing must be said to agitate
her. Everything possible must be kept from her. Dr.
Lange told me last night her heart is more and more
uncertain. And she's getting—well, queer. Ann packed
that tea set, and soon as we turned our backs she unpacked it.

LOUISE (*who is looking through articles in a small cab-
inet, left, rear*)

Oh I hope she doesn't get too queer. We've had enough.
I hate the idea of people thinking we're different.

EBEN

Nothing very funny about an old lady, who's lived

alone too long, getting a bit childish. She'll be all right, once she's up at father's.

STANHOPE

It's important to keep telling her she must do it for me. Don't let her think we feel she isn't able to live down here alone. Tell her I'm alone.

EBEN (*sympathetically*)

Yes. (*Looking around.*) Hate like the dickens to see the place go, Father.

STANHOPE

Do you think I don't?

EBEN

The fun we used to have down here as kids—Elsa and I. Especially when Alison was here. Remember how she was always making us presents?

STANHOPE

I remember.

EBEN

An apple—pebbles from the river—little cakes she'd baked. And always her jolly little verses with them. "Alison won't tell," she'd say, when Elsa and I had run off to the river. "Alison knows," she'd say.

TED (*repeating softly as he writes*)

Alison knows.

EBEN

It was all so darn real today, coming down here for the last time. And the century going—her century.

When I got the first glimpse of the place through the trees I had a feeling of the whole century being piled on top of her, that she couldn't get out from under.

LOUISE

How *morbid.* Don't *let* your mind run on such things!

EBEN

Who am I—to tell my mind where to run? You know, Father, I'd like to hear her say once more—right now —here—Alison understands, because—I'll be darned if I do.

TED

Was Alison a virgin?

LOUISE

Father!

STANHOPE

See here now!

EBEN

Getting fresh, aren't you?

TED

It isn't me. Why won't you understand? *He* wants to *know*—and I got to make this grade.

STANHOPE

There is such a thing as taste, young man.

TED

Just what I told him—women of one's family—and he almost slapped me. Well, was she a virgin?

STANHOPE (*violently*)

Yes!

TED

Oh, gee, I hoped she wasn't. (*Starting to write, turning.*) How do you know?

STANHOPE

Leave the room!

TED

Where'll I go? I don't see how you can be sure—

EBEN (*going to him, taking him by the collar, lifting him to his feet and shaking him back and forth*)

You miserable little fool! And you're the baby Alison used to say got through from heaven. The hell you did! Didn't you get *anything* from her? (*Shaking him.*) Didn't you?

TED

Say! Leave me alone, will you? I guess I was only two years old when she died! What do I know about her?

EBEN

Nothing. Absolutely nothing, and never will. Why that prof ought to kill you. If your soul wasn't a shriveled peanut something from her would have made you a human being!

STANHOPE

Come now, Eben. That's enough.

EBEN

What's the use of having had an Alison in the family?

Sometimes I think I'll run away from all this—and find her.

LOUISE

You haven't been drinking, have you?

EBEN

No, but I will.

LOUISE

If you haven't been drinking there's even less excuse for this raving.

EBEN

You think it's raving, Father?

STANHOPE

I think it is too uncontrolled.

EBEN

The last day we'll ever be in her house—the last day it will be her house—how can we help but think of her —and feel her—and wonder what's the matter with us—that something from her didn't—oh Lord, *make* us something!

[ELSA, *wearing coat, furs, hat, has stepped inside the door. She has beauty, a soft radiance.*

ELSA (*in low thrilling voice*)

Yes, Eben. Yes!

EBEN

Elsa!

STANHOPE

Elsa!

ELSA

Father, may I—come in?
[*One hand, palm up. Goes out toward him, timidly, but eloquent.*

LOUISE

Certainly you may not—not while—
[*But is afraid to go on,* STANHOPE *is staring so strangely at his daughter.*

TED

Hello, Elsa. How'd you get here?

ELSA (*gratefully*)

Hello, Ted. (*To her father.*) Perhaps I shouldn't have come. But Eben wrote me the place was being broken up and—

LOUISE

You wrote to her?

EBEN

Yes, I write to my sister.

ELSA

I had to be here once more. I thought—perhaps it's too much to ask—but I hoped you would let me stay here. Just tonight. It would—do me good.

LOUISE (*with a shrill laugh*)

Now that's—*funny.*
[*Laughs again.*

ELSA (*advancing a little to her father*)

It doesn't mean you forgive me, Father, if—if you

don't. If you can't. But won't you just do it—because
Alison would do it? She'd take my hands. She'd say—
Little Elsa. She'd say—Elsa has come home.
[*From upstairs a wild cry from* JENNIE.

JENNIE (*above*)

Mr. Stanhope—everybody!—help!
[EBEN *hurries out.*

JENNIE (*off*)

Everybody—quick—the house—burning!

TED

Fire! I smelled it!
[*He runs out,* LOUISE *goes, and* ANN. STANHOPE *does
not pass his daughter without pausing a moment,
looking at her.*
[*Outside a confusion of voices, a running about. Only*
ELSA *remains as she was, as if she cannot move.*

ELSA

Just as I stepped into the house. As if—as if— (*Shaking this off.*) Oh, no—no. (*She looks around the room.
Softly.*) Don't burn. Don't.
[*After another moment, having looked from one thing
to another, she goes to the books, runs her hand over
them. Stands there. But at a noise of something falling upstairs, she becomes frightened, suddenly takes
an armful of books. Is starting out, but stopped by a
confident shout from* EBEN.

EBEN (*off*)

It's all right. We're getting it! Two more buckets,
Ted!

[ELSA *sits down where* ANN *had sat, still holding the books, bent over them, her back to the door.*

[*After a moment* AGATHA *comes in.* ELSA *does not hear her, and* AGATHA, *in a curious, fixed state has not seen* ELSA. *She sits where she sat before. She is white, rigid.* ELSA, *moving a little, drops one of the books.*

AGATHA (*not turning*)

What's that? Who's here?

ELSA

Aunt Agatha!

AGATHA (*still not turning, as if she can not*)

Who's that? Who's here? (ELSA *goes to her, and as still* AGATHA *does not look up, sits on a stool beside her.*) Elsa.

ELSA

Yes—Elsa.

AGATHA

Elsa went away.

ELSA

She came back. (*Timidly.*) Are you—glad?

AGATHA

Alison was so afraid of fire.

TED (*off*)

That fixes it!

ELSA

They are getting the fire out.

AGATHA

No. Burning. All burning. All at once.

ELSA (*trying to take her hand*)

No, Aunt Agatha. You see the boys are here. They are getting the fire out. There's nothing to be afraid of.

AGATHA

I am not afraid—now.

STANHOPE (*outside*)

Agatha! Where is she?
[ELSA *starts up, but* AGATHA *takes her hand in a fierce grip, forcing her down.*

STANHOPE (*still off*)

Jennie! Where's Miss Agatha? Agatha!

ELSA (*freeing herself, going to the door*)

Here, Father. Aunt Agatha is in here with me.
[STANHOPE *comes in.*

STANHOPE (*gently, as he sees her there rigid, white*)

It's all right, Agatha. Just a little blaze. Nothing whatever to worry about. The boys have it out already. (*After staring at him,* AGATHA *leans back with a wail that goes into a whimper.*) You understand, don't you, Agatha? They have put the fire out.

AGATHA (*with horror*)

They have put the fire out.
[*Enter* EBEN, *coat off, flushed, much excited.*

EBEN

That fire was set, Father.

STANHOPE

What?

EBEN

We found the charred straw—in the closet that breaks through to Alison's room—coal oil there—and in Alison's room. Some one was trying to burn the house.

STANHOPE

But that's—incredible. *Why?* Oh, no—you're mistaken.

EBEN

It's undeniable. The evidence is right there.

STANHOPE (*going to the door*)

Jennie! (AGATHA *leans away, as if avoiding something.* ELSA *holds her hands.*) Jennie! (*Turning.*) I don't believe a word of it! (*Enter* JENNIE.) What do you know about this fire?

JENNIE (*distraught, almost crying*)

I don't know anything about it. I smelled the smoke. I ran up. It was burning—in the closet.
[*Enter* LOUISE.

LOUISE

The fire was set. Some one tried to burn the house.

STANHOPE (*to* JENNIE)

Who's been here?

JENNIE

Nobody. Nobody. Just the family—and me—and Michael.

STANHOPE

Who's been upstairs?

LOUISE

That reporter was upstairs.

STANHOPE

Why you've all lost your wits! What possible reason?

LOUISE

But no other stranger was upstairs.
[STANHOPE *looks at her a moment, incredulous, dazed. Starts for the door.* ANN *comes in.*

STANHOPE

Ann, what do you know about this reporter?

ANN

Why, I don't know anything about him.

LOUISE

Perhaps it isn't a reporter. Perhaps it's—some hostility to the family.

STANHOPE (*angrily*)

That is ridiculous.

LOUISE

Well, who did it? Why?

STANHOPE

How did the fellow seem to you?

ANN

He seemed all right. I thought he was—just what he said he was. I'm sure he's all right. He showed me a poem he had written.

LOUISE

As if that proves anything! Had you known him before?

ANN (*indignant at the tone*)

I had never seen him before.

STANHOPE (*going to the door. Sharply*)

Ted!

TED (*from above*)

Staying up here to make sure!

STANHOPE

Leave Michael on watch. Come down here at once!

EBEN

I can't make head or tail of it. Who would want to burn the house?

ANN (*distressed*)

Mightn't it have just—happened?

LOUISE (*scornfully*)

"Happened?" Straw—saturated with kerosene?
[*Enter* TED.

STANHOPE

Now what about you and this reporter?

TED

Well, what about us?

STANHOPE

Answer my question!

TED

What question, Father? What about us?

STANHOPE

You were the only people in that part of the house—
and a fire was set.

TED

For—Pete's—sake! Talk about *me* being crazy! You
think I set a fire to burn the house?

STANHOPE (*violently*)

No! I don't think anything of the kind! But what did
you do up there?

TED

We looked at Aunt Alison's room. And he talked
about her that crazy way people do talk about her.
And that's all.

STANHOPE

Did you have any straw up there?

TED (*tolerantly*)

Oh, Father, what would I be doing with straw?

STANHOPE (*furiously*)

I don't know what you'd be doing with straw! You

just might have had some idea of making yourself useful!

TED

Useful enough to burn the house.

STANHOPE

Be still! (*Turning to* JENNIE *who stands by the door,
frightened.*) Who had straw upstairs?

JENNIE

Nobody. Nobody's I know of.

STANHOPE

Did you take coal oil upstairs?

JENNIE (*beginning to cry*)

I did not. I did not take coal oil upstairs.

STANHOPE

Very well, Jennie. I believe you. But who—
[*In looking around, bewildered, his eye falls on the
tea set. Slowly he moves over to it, then looks at his
sister, who is still in that strange, fixed state. An idea
comes to him that is a shock. Ponders, incredulous, but
the idea is growing.*

STANHOPE (*to* EBEN)

Straw—you say? (*Moves nearer* AGATHA. *Speaks
gently.*) Agatha, why did you unpack the tea set,
after Ann had packed it for you?

JENNIE

Oh!
[*All look at her. She goes from the room.*

AGATHA

What? What's that you say? Tea set?

STANHOPE

Yes. Why did you unpack it, after Ann had packed it for you?

AGATHA

I can pack my own mother's tea set, can't I?

STANHOPE (*gently*)

But you let her do it for you. (*Silence, after which he speaks carefully.*) Agatha, what did you do with the straw the dishes were packed in?

AGATHA (*as a wail*)

O-h! I wish you'd all go away—and leave me here alone! Why couldn't you *let it burn?*

STANHOPE (*slowly*)

You love the house so much you would *burn* it—rather than—leave it?

AGATHA (*not speaking to any of them now*)

What could I *do?* I tried—and tried. Burn them? All by themselves? (*In a whisper.*) It was—too lonely. [*She falls back.*

STANHOPE

Get brandy, quick. And the doctor. [LOUISE *goes out, and* TED.

AGATHA (*resolutely sitting up*)

I don't want the doctor. [*But she again falls back.*

ELSA

Are you all right, Aunt Agatha?

AGATHA (*looking up at* ELSA)

Couldn't take them away—and couldn't—*couldn't*—

CURTAIN

ACT TWO

ACT TWO

*Scene: The scene is as Act I. It is the same day, three
o'clock in the afternoon.* ANN *is at her typewriter,* STAN-
HOPE *at the table, on which is a box of papers. He crumples the one he was looking at, throws it to the floor,
where there is a heap of discarded papers. He takes some
of them to the fireplace, stands watching them burn.*

STANHOPE (*turning*)

Well, we must get on with it. (*Sitting down, examines
another paper.*) Receipt for a carriage, twenty-eight
years old. People used to keep everything. (*Crumples
it, throws it to the floor.*) I sometimes took your
mother driving in that carriage.

ANN

You were so good to Mother.

STANHOPE (*softly, with a sigh*)

I hope so. (*After a moment of dreaming.*) Remember
how she used to come toward you—her hands out?

ANN (*her hands out*)

I can see them.

STANHOPE

And sitting by the fire, in the blue velvet dress, in
that chair she liked—

ANN

Chippendale.

STANHOPE

Leaning back a little, yet erect, her hands, so long
and white, loosely clasped on an arm of it.

ANN

I can see her.

STANHOPE

You look like her, Ann.

ANN

Not so good-looking.

STANHOPE (*smiling*)

Not quite. But who could be?

ANN

It will be nine years in January.

STANHOPE

Nine years. (*With an effort coming from this, hand-
ing her a package of old papers.*) Just make the lists
of what these deeds are, keep the latest one of each
and put the others in an envelop marked Old Deeds.
[EBEN *enters carrying a large box.*

EBEN

This finishes in the attic. Seems to be mostly old newspapers.

STANHOPE (*taking one*)

James G. Blaine.

EBEN (*who is looking at another*)

Why the old hotel was standing then. The one that burned when I was a kid. Remember going to the fire. (*Turning a page, laughing.*) Did you know the Baileys had sued the McMasters—about stealing a stallion for breeding?

STANHOPE

That stallion was in the courts a long time.

EBEN

And now the McMasters are worth—more than we'll ever see. Shall we keep these?

STANHOPE

Where?

EBEN

I don't know. I think they ought to stay right here. That everything should stay where it is.

STANHOPE

Don't start that again. Don't you think it's harder for me than you? I was born here. Grew up here.

EBEN

That's why. And Alison.

STANHOPE

And Agatha. She can't be left here any longer. You can see that now. And she won't go while we keep the place. Too bad we got that fire out.

EBEN

That was a funny thing. Aunt Agatha must be— pretty bad—trying that with us all right here.

STANHOPE

She kept talking about anything else being too lonely.

EBEN

I think she had something she wanted to burn, and couldn't.

STANHOPE

Yes.

EBEN

What?

STANHOPE

I don't know. Just some old thing she cherished, and didn't want to take from the house.

EBEN

Something about Alison?

STANHOPE

Perhaps.

EBEN

Father, we did publish all the poems, didn't we?

STANHOPE

We gave them all to Professor Burroughs. He took all except a few he thought weren't so good. Those I have, as you know.

EBEN

Letters from Alison, perhaps.

STANHOPE

Each of us has his own. Agatha has the letters Alison

wrote to her. They're not many, for they were so
seldom apart. Of course if she wants to burn her own
letters, she has that right. Though I wish she wouldn't.
She should leave them to the children.

EBEN

Seems very strange to me.

STANHOPE

Yes. Well, it's just because she has become strange.
The Centennial Exposition—1876. Oh we can't burn
these papers. They've been kept too long. Save them
for the children.

EBEN

We're keeping more now than we know where to put.

STANHOPE

Louise can find a place for them. Tomorrow these
will be the newspapers of a former century.

EBEN

You going up to the dance, Ann?

ANN (*shaking her head*)

No.

STANHOPE (*putting down his paper*)

Why I never thought of the dance. Of course you must
go, Ann.

ANN

There's so much to do here. I'd rather help.

EBEN

Turned Walter down, didn't you?

STANHOPE

What's that? Have you quarreled with Walter?

ANN

No, I didn't quarrel with him. I just got tired hearing how fast he could run.

STANHOPE

Ted's going up with the Logans. You go with them, and go to the dance with Ted.

ANN

Ted's taking May McMasters.

STANHOPE

Sometimes I think that boy hasn't a grain of sense. But it's New Year's Eve. You must go to the dance.

ANN (*smiling*)

Please, Mr. Stanhope, if you don't mind my staying here, to begin early in the morning—

EBEN

Shouldn't have given Walter the sack till he was starting back to New Haven.

ANN

I didn't give him the sack. We just decided to run in different directions.

STANHOPE

But aren't you and Louise going to the dance, Eben?

EBEN (*shaking his head*)

I'm bored with their dances.

STANHOPE

I fear you're bored with too much, son.

EBEN

Fear so. But anyway, with Elsa here—and the last night in the old place—

STANHOPE

It's good of you.

EBEN (*brightly*)

Oh, no.
[STANHOPE *again begins looking through the box of papers on the table.* TED *comes in, sits at the desk, takes his unfinished letter from the pigeon hole, glares at it.*

TED

I'll be flunked.

EBEN (*not looking up from his newspaper*)

Might try a little study, for a change.

TED

Tell me something to tell him, Father.

STANHOPE

Have you begun that again?

TED

About her conservatory. Keeping her flowers warm in winter. How did she keep them warm? (*The others go on with what they are doing.*) Well, how do you keep flowers warm? Do you wrap them in cotton? Straw, maybe. What do you suppose Aunt Agatha wanted to burn the house for?

STANHOPE

Because she is feeble, and very sad.

TED

But I thought she liked the house. (*To* ANN.) Make a good story for that reporter!

EBEN

Run out and find him. Tell him all the news!

TED

He's still around. He's down by the river, walking where Alison walked. He's crazy. Nice, though. What flowers, Father? Geraniums? (*Writes.*) Loved geraniums.

STANHOPE (*so sharply* TED *jumps*)

Edward! You have very little sense of family, or very little sense of anything. But perhaps you have sense enough to know what it would mean if your allowance stopped.

TED

Yes, Father. I have the kind of sense can understand that.

STANHOPE

Very well then! No stories about the family—about the fire—to this reporter—or your teacher—or any one else.

TED

You don't know my situation, Father. It's dark. (*Returns to his letter; turns, meekly.*) It's all right

to write about flowers, isn't it? (*Turning back to the letter.*) Violets.
[*Begins to sing "Every morn I bring thee violets." There are voices in the hall.* JENNIE *enters.*

JENNIE

Mr. and Mrs. Hodges are here.

STANHOPE (*low, with irritation*)

They weren't to come again until we were out of the house.

EBEN

Send them away.

STANHOPE (*decisively, after hesitation*)

No. Perhaps we can close the deal. Very well, Jennie. Ask them to come in. (*She goes.*) But Agatha mustn't know.

EBEN

She's still lying down in her room.

STANHOPE

Who's with her?

EBEN

Elsa.

TED

How do you spell mignonette?

EBEN

F-o-o-l.

TED

That spells E-b-e-n.

[*Enter* MR. *and* MRS. HODGES. *He is a small, lean, shrewd-faced man. His wife is larger and has a big rather foolish face.*

HODGES

Well! How'd do, everybody.

STANHOPE

How do you do, Mr. Hodges? How are you today, Mrs. Hodges?

MRS. HODGES

Oh, I keep going.
[EBEN *brings a chair for her.*

HODGES

Well, guess you weren't expecting us.

STANHOPE

No, not today.

HODGES

Like to decide between this place and another we got in mind. Other's in better repair.

EBEN

Then you'd better take that one.

HODGES

Well, I dunno. My wife kind of turns to this one. Thinks she could fix it up pretty—woman's notions.

MRS. HODGES

I think with piazzas down stairs and up it would be nice for my summer boarders.

STANHOPE (*rather faintly*)
Summer boarders?

HODGES
That's how we calculate. Don't think a poor man like me'd buy this ramshackle old place for just my old woman and those two young uns, do you? But we'd have to fix it all up. Paint her a bright yellow, maybe, with green edgin'—somethin' you can *see*. Summer boarders wouldn't take to a gray house edged with red you can't tell for red.

MRS. HODGES
I could make that conservatory into a sun parlor where they could sit when it rained.

HODGES
But 'twould mean a big outlay, 'cause we'd have to cut it up in more rooms.
[*The* STANHOPES *are silent.*

MRS. HODGES (*feeling she must break the pause*)
Nobody could pay what'd be right to pay for rooms that big.

HODGES
Well, folks don't need rooms so big now.

MRS. HODGES
Hard to take care of.

HODGES
But it's in bad repair, Mr. Stanhope.

STANHOPE (*with effort*)

Oh, I don't think so. The roof needs just a little mending, but the foundations are good.

MRS. HODGES

Looks a good deal run down, Mr. Stanhope. (*Fearing she has been impolite.*) Of course you haven't been living here yourself. You have your nice place in town. But for summer boarders 'twould need a lot of paint and varnish, and that new wall-paper that's more lively like.

HODGES

All those things cost. They cost.

STANHOPE

Certainly. But we feel our price is low. The house has —character.

HODGES

Character. (*Rubbing his chin.*) Well, maybe so. But *what* character? Not the character for summer boarders. That's what I tell the old lady here. And how do I know there'd be any boarders?

EBEN (*cheerfully*)

There might not.

HODGES

Just what I say. Folks like to go up the river now-a-days, not down the river. And with the old Mississippi rising higher every year, seems like she'd wash this place away 'fore we could get dead and buried.

EBEN

Then you could have a house boat.

HODGES

How? (*Laughs loudly.*) Yes, that's a joke. (*To his wife.*) Summer boarders on a house boat.

STANHOPE (*courteous, but cold*)

Just why did you come in today, Mr. Hodges?

HODGES

Want to take one more look at her, 'fore we give her up. Try to figure out where we could put in partitions—modernize. Outside, too—needs a lot. Too many trees makes a place gloomy.

EBEN

Those trees have been growing a long time.

HODGES

Well, then they've been growing long enough, haven't they? (*Laughing, waiting for* EBEN *to join him, but* EBEN *does not.*) And that lilac hedge—shuts the place in too much. What's the use putting your money in a place nobody can see? Take out some of that tangled old stuff and put in flower beds in fancy shapes— heart-shaped, maybe—you'd be surprised the difference it would make.

EBEN (*softly*)

No, I wouldn't be surprised. (*Speaking more brightly.*) Now here's an interesting thing, Mr. Hodges. You aren't sure you want to buy, and we aren't sure we want to sell.

HODGES (*to* STANHOPE, *sharply*)

Not want to sell? But you made me a proposition, and I've gone to the expense of getting a carpenter to figure on it.

STANHOPE

I will stand by what I said. But you will have to make up your minds. We have other possibilities for the place.

HODGES

Now there you surprise me, Mr. Stanhope. You certainly do surprise me. And I'm very much afraid you'd be disappointed in those other parties. Don't think anybody else 'd be fool enough to buy it. Now that's my opinion, if you want my opinion. Know darn well I wouldn't buy it, 'cept my old woman's got the idea, and when a woman gets an idea, you might as well give up.

STANHOPE

I think Mrs. Hodges' idea is—practical.

MRS. HODGES (*nodding and smiling*)

They could go out in row boats. Take their lunch over to the Island, and that would get them out of the house, part of the time.

EBEN

I think you'd make more leaving the house as it is, and getting people who would—

STANHOPE (*low*)

Never mind, Eben.

HODGES

No. No, there you're wrong, young man. Summer boarders want things modern, and cheerful. But I tell you what bothers me, Mr. Stanhope. The place ain't healthy.

STANHOPE

I grew up here. I'm healthy.

HODGES

Seems like the river had something against this place. Right here on this bend's where she washes in more and more.

EBEN

Yes, Mr. Hodges, I really think you would die of rheumatism, shortly before you were drowned.

HODGES

How? (*Laughing.*) He jokes, don't he? Well, my brother Ed used to joke. Never could figure out what Ed was getting at.

STANHOPE

I can't figure out just what you are getting at, Mr. Hodges. We are very busy here today. Do you want the place, or not?

HODGES

Well, now, that depends.

STANHOPE

You weren't coming again until we had left the house.

HODGES

That's right—so we weren't. But the carpenter's coming Friday—make an estimate. Like to look it over once more ourselves, get a few ideas of our own, for I know damn well—excuse me, Miss— (*Bending over to nod to* ANN, *who has been going ahead with her work.*)—what he'll try to do.

EBEN (*softly*)

Yes. Carpenters are very expensive now.

HODGES

They are that. So we'll just have a look at them upstairs rooms, Mr. Stanhope. See how we can portion 'em out.

MR. STANHOPE

I am sorry not to fall in with your plans, but my sister is up there, and she is ill.

MRS. HODGES

That so? Miss Stanhope ailing? Well, she's—getting along, isn't she?

STANHOPE

Yes. She is.

HODGES

Well, we all got to get old some time. That's what I say. No use to fret.

MRS. HODGES

We wouldn't ask to go in her room, Mr. Stanhope. And

we'd keep quiet—just whisper. I have sick headaches,
myself.

STANHOPE (*giving up, after considering*)

I suppose it can't be helped. Will you go with them,
Eben?

EBEN

Awfully busy here.

STANHOPE

Ted! No, Ann, please. And very quietly, that I ask
you.

MRS. HODGES (*in a whisper, and tip-toeing*)

We'll go—like this.
[*Exit the* HODGES, *with* ANN.

EBEN

I don't think we could possibly do worse.

STANHOPE

I don't think we could do better.

EBEN

They'll destroy it.

STANHOPE

I want it destroyed.

EBEN (*coldly*)

You do? I care for it.

STANHOPE

I care for it so much I don't want—itself, to go to
some one else.

EBEN

That sounds more like Aunt Agatha than you, Father.

STANHOPE

Very well. Agatha and I are the only two left. Listen now! Ted! Leave that foolishness! Try and do something with your own brains—not trading on your Aunt Alison! Are you listening?

TED

Yes, sir.

STANHOPE

And don't ask me how to spell anything!

TED

No, sir.

STANHOPE

Some day, when I'm gone, you'll talk about this again, and wonder why I sold it, and blame me. And perhaps you'll be right, but I'm using the best judgment I've got. Agatha can not be left here. Her heart's feeble, and her mind—not what it was. If the place remained, she'd come back here, and you know it as well as I do.

EBEN

She couldn't be left here—with a nurse?

STANHOPE

That might be all right about her heart. Not her mind.

EBEN

She's old to transplant.

STANHOPE

And we're not doing it well. All the confusion. And now—Elsa.

EBEN

She loves Elsa. Elsa doesn't harm anybody—except herself.

STANHOPE

She harmed all of us. She disgraced us.

EBEN

Maybe she couldn't help it.

STANHOPE

"Couldn't help it"! What a weak defense. Alison helped it—and so did I.

EBEN

What did you say, Father?

STANHOPE

Never mind what I said. The only person in this family who has any sense of family is Louise—and she's another family.

EBEN

Oh Louise takes it too hard.

STANHOPE

She goes at it wrong, but she's the only one wants what I want.

TED (*hopefully entering the conversation*)
And what is that, Father?

STANHOPE

Hold a family together. Have some pride.

TED

I got a great idea. Redeem family fortune. Fellow at school's worked out a new idea for putting on rubber tires. Like to go in with him, soon 's our sentence expires at Cambridge.

STANHOPE

You will go in your father's office, which was his father's before him, and you will try and show more interest in the business than your brother does.

TED

Sometimes I think I haven't just the mind that makes a lawyer.

EBEN

Oh, I think you have.

STANHOPE

What do you mean? The law is a noble profession.

TED

Thought I might do better in some kind of a rubber wheel business.

EBEN

I tell you, Father, suppose I take a year off.

STANHOPE

Seems to me you've taken ten years off.

EBEN

Sometimes I feel I want something else.

STANHOPE

What?

EBEN

I don't know.

STANHOPE

And what about your family?

EBEN

Oh that's why I'm going.

STANHOPE

You are not going!

EBEN

Probably not.

STANHOPE

Going where?

EBEN

I don't know. Somewhere—where things are different.

STANHOPE

Things are not different anywhere.

EBEN

Sometimes I think if I didn't have to do anything for a while—I could do something.

STANHOPE

What?

EBEN

Don't know yet.

STANHOPE

You have your children.

EBEN

Louise's.

STANHOPE

Well, you couldn't very well have had them alone, could you? Come, Eben, don't talk like a weakling. What if you aren't perfectly happy with Louise? I wasn't happy with your mother, either, but I didn't run away, leaving my children to shift for themselves.

EBEN

It isn't just Louise—or, I suppose not. It's things I used to think about when I was with Alison. And still think about—when she's with me.

STANHOPE

Alison didn't desert her family.

EBEN

No, but I don't write poetry.

STANHOPE

Oh, dear.

EBEN

Never mind, Father—guess I'm just talking foolishly, because the old place is being broken up.

STANHOPE

It's a time to put your shoulder to the wheel.

EBEN

All right. Where's the wheel?

STANHOPE

Here.
[*Pushing toward him the box of papers on the table.*
[EBEN *begins on these, his father too has taken out a handful of them.*

TED (*after crumpling a sheet of his letter*)

Tell you what, Eben, I got an idea.

EBEN

Doubt it.

TED

You do something for me, I'll do something for you.

EBEN

What?

TED

Well, give you an interest in taking off rubber tires.

EBEN

Thanks. Got too many interests already. (*Showing a paper to his father.*) This any good?

TED

Well, I'll run away with Louise.

EBEN

That's better.

STANHOPE

Don't talk such nonsense.

TED

> Kidnap her. And you write me a theme—about Alison. I'm two behind. "Alison knows" you could call it.

EBEN

> So I could.

TED

> Just write the way you talk. Sounds funny in talk, but written it would look all right.

EBEN (*with a real interest, which makes his father look at him*)

> Do you think so?

TED

> About the little presents, and—oh the things she used to say to you. How she looked—and moved around—and why she was different from other folks.

EBEN

> I would like to do that.

TED

> Fine! Dandy!

STANHOPE

> Did you ever try to write, Eben?

EBEN

> I used to write things—and show them to Alison.

STANHOPE

> I never knew that.

EBEN

> No. No one else knew—except Elsa.

STANHOPE

And did you keep it up?

EBEN

Not after I was married.

TED

It's a bargain! You help me get through college, and I'll put you on your feet—financially speaking, on your feet.

EBEN (*thinking of something else*)

Thanks, awfully.

TED

Don't mention it.
[*Enter* LOUISE.

LOUISE

Elsa isn't staying here, is she?

STANHOPE

Tonight.

LOUISE

Then I'm not staying.

EBEN

Family feeling.

LOUISE

Exactly. I'm sorry, Father Stanhope, but I can't stay in the house with Elsa. She ran away with the husband of my best friend, leaving—

EBEN

Father knows just what she did, Louise.

LOUISE

How could I ever face Margaret again, if I'd stayed under the roof with Elsa?

EBEN

Monstrous idea—staying under the roof with Elsa.

LOUISE

I am sorry to say it is.

STANHOPE

And I am sorry, Louise, but in that case you will have to go up with the Logans and Ted.

LOUISE

I don't think I should be the one to be turned out!

STANHOPE

I am not turning you out; but neither am I turning Elsa out—not tonight.

LOUISE

Was there any reason for her coming—other than to make trouble?

STANHOPE

She felt there was a reason, apparently.

TED

And I'm glad she came. Why shouldn't she?

LOUISE

Yes—indeed—why shouldn't she! Much you know about it—or care—what the town says. It will be known she's here, and just stir it all up!

EBEN

This isn't very pleasant for Father, Louise.

LOUISE

Did I create the situation?

EBEN

You seem to be creating this one.

LOUISE

I am sorry for Father—sorrier than any one. But there is nothing to do about Elsa except condemn her.

EBEN

The Logans are coming at four, aren't they, Ted?

LOUISE

You side with her—against me, your wife?

EBEN

You take too much pleasure in siding against her. She's had enough, hasn't she?

LOUISE

She brought it on herself.

EBEN

If you're so thick with Margaret, might persuade her to be decent enough to get a divorce.

LOUISE

She does not believe in divorce. She is standing by her principles.

EBEN

She is standing by her thirst for revenge.

LOUISE

Oh, of course you think *she's* the one in the wrong! You think—

STANHOPE

Don't quarrel, children. Elsa did wrong—Louise is right there. But I am not turning her out—not tonight.

LOUISE

Then I go.

EBEN (*cheerfully*)

Goodbye.

LOUISE

A husband should be loyal to his wife!

EBEN

Who says so?

LOUISE

Now you're talking foolishly again! As if you hadn't good sense. Every one says so—every one.

EBEN (*after turning a paper*)

No they don't.

LOUISE

But they *do*. A husband should be loyal to his wife. Isn't that so, Father Stanhope?

STANHOPE

Certainly.

EBEN

Why "certainly," Father? If a wife steals—murders—

LOUISE

Steals? Murders? Do I steal—murder?
[*She waits for a reply which does not come.*

TED

Tell you what, Louise, let's you and me take a little
trip. (LOUISE *can only stare.*) Take you to Cambridge with me. Quite a good deal going on. You'd
probably like it.

LOUISE (*slowly, to* STANHOPE)

I just don't know what to make of this family. I do
not know what to make of them.

EBEN

You can't make anything of them, Louise. I think the
idea of a little trip with Ted—

STANHOPE (*bringing down his hand*)

Stop that nonsense!

LOUISE (*observing* HODGES' *cap and muffler on the chair*)

Who is here?

STANHOPE

The Hodges.

LOUISE

Where are they?

STANHOPE

They are looking over the house.

LOUISE

Who's with them? Who is showing them round?

STANHOPE

Ann.

LOUISE

Ann? But why Ann? Why an outsider?

STANHOPE

Oh I don't consider Ann an outsider.

LOUISE (*forcing herself to speak respectfully*)

But she is an outsider, Father Stanhope. She's your secretary. She's not a member of the family. (*After a silence.*) Is she?

STANHOPE

She is as dear to me as my own daughter. Well—no, not that.

LOUISE (*gently*)

Of course, Father, I know Elsa can't be dear to you —now.

STANHOPE

Elsa is dear to me, though I've lost her.

EBEN

Don't say that, Father.

STANHOPE

Isn't it true?

LOUISE

You have me, Father.

STANHOPE

Yes. Yes, thank you, Louise.
[*There are voices on the stairs. The* HODGES *enter.* ANN *leaving them at the door.*

LOUISE (*capably taking hold of things*)

How do you do, Mrs. Hodges? Though perhaps you don't know me. I am Mrs. Eben Stanhope.

MRS. HODGES

How'd do, Mrs. Stanhope.

HODGES

Pleased to meet you, mam.

LOUISE

Of course you are seeing the house in great confusion. But we'll have everything out of here soon.

MRS. HODGES

Oh, that's all right.

HODGES

Quite a chore—moving.

LOUISE

It's a *dear* old place, isn't it?

HODGES

Well, we think it's dear enough.
[*Looks slyly at* EBEN.

LOUISE

So roomy, and well built. And such *traditions*.

HODGES

How?

MRS. HODGES

It's for my summer boarders—if we take it.

LOUISE

Now Mrs. Hodges, I think that's an *excellent* idea. So

practical. Do you know, I've thought the same thing myself. It's really too big for a family, but for summer boarders—right here on the river—the woods all around. Quite likely I can send you some people.

MRS. HODGES

Oh *that* would be nice.

HODGES

Right clever of you, mam.

LOUISE

And that big cheerful kitchen to cook for them! I wonder how many people used to be cooked for in that kitchen, Father?

STANHOPE

A good many.

LOUISE

And now again the house will be full of people having a good time. That's a nice idea for us, too, isn't it, Father? (STANHOPE *tries to reply, but does not speak.*) You see we love the house. It's a real grief to us, giving it up. But it's too big for a family. That's why we're letting you have it.

HODGES (*slyly*)

Very good of you, mam.

EBEN

Quite philanthropic.

HODGES

How? (*Bursting out laughing.*) He jokes, don't he?

LOUISE

Yes. Jokes.

STANHOPE (*abruptly*)

Do you want the house, Hodges?

HODGES

Yes.

STANHOPE (*who seems stunned*)

Good. (*With effort.*) Sign up for it now?

HODGES (*sitting down at the table, taking out his check book*)

Bind the bargain.

STANHOPE (*resolutely*)

Good. Then come in the office—tomorrow's New Year's
—come Thursday, and we'll go over the deed. You'll
find everything in order.

LOUISE (*to* MRS. HODGES)

You see there are no complications. The place has
been in the family from the first.

[STANHOPE *is staring ahead, and does not see the
check* HODGES *holds out to him.*

HODGES

A hundred fifty. That all right?

STANHOPE

Yes. Quite all right.

HODGES

Well, now we'll be out of your way. Soon's you go out,
we come in.

STANHOPE

Very good.

LOUISE

And I know you're going to enjoy it—just as much as we did.

MRS. HODGES

You must come to see us sometime.

LOUISE

Indeed we will.

HODGES

Guess you won't hardly know the old place, once we take hold.

MRS. HODGES

We're going to paint—modernize.

LOUISE

That's just what it needs.

HODGES

Well, Thursday then.

STANHOPE

Thursday.

HODGES

How's ten?

STANHOPE

Let us say ten. (*Rising.*) Goodday, Mrs. Hodges.

MRS. HODGES

Goodday, Mr. Stanhope. And I hope your sister will find herself more smart for the moving.

STANHOPE

Thank you. I hope so.

HODGES

Well, 'bye folks. (*To* EBEN, *laughing.*) Couldn't crack another joke, could you?

EBEN

Couldn't possibly.

HODGES (*to* LOUISE)

Always nice to have a cheerful member of the family.

LOUISE

Yes, isn't it nice?
[LOUISE *starts out with them.*

HODGES

We go out the back way. Got the team there.
[STANHOPE, *sinking to his chair, holds the check, staring at it.*

EBEN (*bitterly*)

So that ends—
[*But observing his father, doesn't go on.*

TED

Well, so it's sold. Gee! Now it isn't ours any more. What you getting for it, Father?
[*His father does not seem to hear.*
[*Enter* JENNIE.

JENNIE

He's here again.

EBEN

Who?

JENNIE

Him. That reporter that didn't set fire to the house.

EBEN

We can't see a reporter now.

JENNIE

It isn't you he wants. It's Miss Ann.

STANHOPE (*sharply*)

What for?

KNOWLES (*stepping inside the door*)

Afraid I'll have to explain that myself. Only, well, you see—(*Confused*). Awfully sorry to bother you, but what else could I do?

[JENNIE, *wanting to linger, is putting to rights some things on the window seat.*

STANHOPE

I can think of a number of other things you might have done.

KNOWLES (*smiling*)

What?

STANHOPE

Gone back to Chicago.

KNOWLES

Without seeing her, you mean?

STANHOPE

But why do you wish to see Miss Leslie?

KNOWLES

Is *that* her name?

STANHOPE

That is her name, but you haven't said why you wish
to see her.

KNOWLES (*flushing*)

Well, that's hard to say—to you.

STANHOPE

Then I'm afraid you can't see her.

TED (*in warning voice*)

Be kind, Father. Be kind.

STANHOPE

Anything you wish to ask my secretary you can
ask me.

KNOWLES

Sorry to disagree, Mr. Stanhope, but, really, I can't.

STANHOPE

Something about my sister Alison?

KNOWLES

Well—yes, indirectly.

STANHOPE

Oh we've had enough of that.

KNOWLES

I haven't.

STANHOPE

We are unable to give you more time.

KNOWLES

But excuse me again, it isn't your time I want.

TED

You'll just have to tell him straight out. When people get older they have to be told.

STANHOPE (*angrily*)

Is that so?

TED

Yes, sir.

KNOWLES

It hasn't anything to do with the paper.

STANHOPE

Then I understand it even less.

KNOWLES

I wanted to ask her to take a walk with me.

STANHOPE

You don't even know her name, and you expect her to take a walk with you?

KNOWLES

I don't expect, exactly. I hope.

TED

There's a difference.

STANHOPE

Indeed?

TED (*meekly*)

Yes, sir.

STANHOPE (*heatedly*)

But why do you want to take a walk with her?

TED

Oh—*gee*. 'Cause he *likes* her. You don't have to know a girl's name to like her.

KNOWLES

No, you don't. Though it's a very nice name, Ann Leslie. It suits her, I think.

STANHOPE (*after looking at him some time*)

Jennie, tell Miss Ann a gentleman is here to see her.
[JENNIE *goes.*

KNOWLES

Thank you, sir. I thought about it a long time, and I didn't know any way to see her, but just walk in and ask for her.

STANHOPE (*who seems confused*)

No doubt it was better than throwing stones at the window.

TED

Or you might have set fire to the house. (*As his father pushes his chair back.*) Well, then she would have run out, wouldn't she?
[*He and* KNOWLES *laugh.*

STANHOPE

Eben, have you decided which books you want to take?
[*They walk over to the books, into the alcove.*

KNOWLES

You know, I think all your family have something of the spirit of Alison Stanhope.

TED

Oh, gee, I don't.

KNOWLES

Yes, coming in fresh, I can tell better than you. It's as if something of her remained here, in you all, in— in quite a different form.

TED

Different, all right.

KNOWLES

A—playfulness.

TED

Golly, you think we're playful? Why man, we're going through the blackest page of our history. As for me, I can't decide which room to choose.

KNOWLES

Choose?

TED

To hang myself.

KNOWLES

The river's handy.

TED

Good swimmer. Can you write themes?

KNOWLES

You bet.

TED

Write one for me—about playfulness, or suicide, or
something, and I'll—I got a lot of influence with Ann.

KNOWLES

Maybe you're in love with her.

TED

No. Always been around the house a lot. Too much
like a sister. Anyway, Ann's pretty old.

KNOWLES

She is not old!

TED

She's twenty-three!

KNOWLES

I'm twenty-five.

TED

Well, then she isn't old for you.

KNOWLES

I'm glad she has this nice position.

TED

It isn't a position.

KNOWLES

What is it then?

TED

Oh it's just—the way it is.
[*Enter* ANN ; TED *returns to his letter, whistling "The
Stars and Stripes."*

KNOWLES

I thought perhaps you'd take a walk with me.

ANN (*startled, confused*)

You did?

KNOWLES

Got my nerve, haven't I?

ANN

Why, I don't know.

TED

Better not go, Ann. You might take cold.

KNOWLES

No theme.

TED (*softly*)

Oh, yes. Clever work. (*Rising.*) Well, I'm not going
to take a walk, thank you just as much. Got to two-
step a hundred miles tonight. (*Goes to the door,
whistling two-step.*) My advice to you, Ann, as one of
your natural protectors, is not to go. What do we
know about this young man? [Never trust anybody
from Chicago.]

KNOWLES

I was born in Grand Rapids.

TED

You see? We hadn't even known where he was born.
And we don't know yet what his grandfather did.

KNOWLES

He made shoes.

TED

    That's why he has to walk. Bum joke.

ANN

    No joke at all.

TED (*sadly*)

    No joke at all.
    [*He goes.*

KNOWLES

    It's true you don't know anything about me. But
how will you ever know, if I don't have a chance to
tell you? Now don't say you don't want to know.

ANN

    I haven't said it.

KNOWLES

    If we don't take a walk now, we'll never take a walk in
this century. Had you thought of that?

ANN

    I hadn't, to tell the truth.
    [EBEN *comes in with an armful of books.*

KNOWLES

    The sun of this century is setting.
    [*He has said it as matter of fact, but is himself caught
into its large implication.* EBEN, *who has put his books
on the table stands, a little bowed, in thought.*

ANN (*softly*)

    Yes.
    [EBEN *goes back into the alcove.*

KNOWLES

I was walking down there by the river. (*While he is speaking* STANHOPE *is seen at the opening of the alcove, his back to them, looking at books. He takes out a small volume, opening it.*) And I didn't know whether I was thinking of Alison Stanhope, or thinking of you. Well, guess you were part of the same thing. And I was thinking of the last day of the century getting dim. (STANHOPE *is listening, though he has not turned.*) You know, how you think of a lot of things at once. I thought of how she used to walk where I was walking. (STANHOPE *turns, though they do not see him.*) And never will again. But it was as if her thoughts were there. They must have been hers—for they were better than mine. And it seemed to me if you would walk there with me—you and I together —well, that she wouldn't be gone. (*Abruptly.*) You think I'm crazy?

ANN

No. No, I don't.

KNOWLES

Perhaps I could even write a poem about it—how the river flowed by the sea, as her century flowed—to eternity.

STANHOPE (*quietly*)

I think a walk might do you good, Ann.

KNOWLES

Thank you, sir.

ANN

Well, just a little walk. I'll get my things.

KNOWLES

Fine!

[*She goes.*

[*Rather timidly, to* STANHOPE *who stands as he was, and holding open the little book.*

It must be hard for you, leaving this old house.

STANHOPE

It is hard. (*He feels the book in his hands, looks at it, looks at the young man, goes to him, holding it out.*) This is a book my sister Alison loved and used.

KNOWLES (*taking it*)

Emerson's Poems. (*Looking through it.*) Did *she* mark it?

[STANHOPE *nods.*

STANHOPE

I was going to take it for myself. But she loved to make her little gifts. So—for her—on the last day of her century—I would like to give it to you.

KNOWLES (*incredulous*)

You *would?* Oh, *thank* you, sir. (*Feeling the book as something precious.*) I can't tell you how— Why, I can hardly believe it! I never in my life heard of anything more generous.

STANHOPE (*a little embarrassed*)

Oh, no; not at all.

KNOWLES (*looking at the book, begins to read aloud what he sees*)

"Hast thou named all the birds without a gun;
    Loved the wood-rose and left it on its stalk;

At rich men's tables eaten bread and pulse;
Unarmed, faced danger with a heart of trust;
And loved so well a high behavior
In man or maid, that thou from speech refrained,
Nobility more nobly to repay?—
O be my friend, and teach me to be thine!"

(*Pause.*) It's called Forbearance.

STANHOPE (*simply*)

Thank you. (*Holds out his hand for the book.*) I will
read you one—because you are a poet.
[*Turns a few pages.*

KNOWLES

I'm afraid—

STANHOPE

It is called "The House."

"There is no architect
    Can build as the muse can;
She is skilful to select
    Materials for her plan;

Slow and warily to choose
    Rafters of immortal pine,
(*He glances up to the beamed ceiling above.*)
    Or cedar incorruptible,
    Worthy her design."

Some other things, and then— (*Looking ahead.*)

"She lays her beams in music,
    In music every one,

To the cadence of the whirling world
Which dances round the sun.

That so they shall not be displaced
By lapses or by wars,
But for the love of happy souls
Outlive the newest stars."

[*He hands back the book.*

KNOWLES

Alison's house.

STANHOPE

Yes.
[EBEN *comes from the alcove with more books.*

EBEN

These all right for me, Father?
[*They look at them,* ANN *returns.*

ANN

All ready.

KNOWLES

Fine! Well—goodbye. And thank you—again.

STANHOPE

Goodbye.

ANN

I'll be back.
[*They laugh, go out.*

EBEN

Did you notice Ann?

STANHOPE

Yes, I noticed her. She never looked more like her mother.

EBEN

Happy.

STANHOPE

She's in love.

EBEN

In *love?* (*Laughing.*) Oh, come, Father! She doesn't know him!

STANHOPE

Neither did Alison know him.

EBEN

It must have been—pretty tough for Alison—giving him up.

STANHOPE

You'll never know. I know a little—no one will ever know the half. Yes, you can have the Plato, and what you want. Who will value them more than you?

EBEN

Shall I ask Aunt Agatha, too?

STANHOPE (*shaking his head*)

What are books to Agatha—now?
[ELSA *comes in.*

EBEN

We're looking through the books. You must take some of them, mustn't she, Father?

STANHOPE

If she likes.

ELSA

Could I have the David Copperfield Alison read
to us?

EBEN (*taking it from the books he has selected*)

Here it is.

ELSA

But you were taking it.

EBEN

I have others. (*Giving it.*) Take it. She read it to us
when you had sprained your ankle jumping from the
hayloft. Remember?

ELSA (*looking through the book*)

I remember. (*Reads on, smiles at something she sees.*)
Aunt Agatha wants to come in here, Father.

STANHOPE

The doctor said she should stay in bed.

ELSA

She won't. She's up, and she says she wants to be down
here.

STANHOPE

Oh, I wish it were tomorrow.

ELSA

Shall I let her come?

STANHOPE

I don't suppose you can stop her. I'll speak to her. [*He goes.*

EBEN

You staying long, Elsa?

ELSA

No. How could I? (EBEN *is silent.*) I suppose I shouldn't have come.

EBEN

Far as I am concerned, you should. Father—

ELSA

He looks so much older.

EBEN

You made him older. Nothing ever hit him as hard.

ELSA

Oh, Eben—don't.

EBEN

Well, you've got to take it.

ELSA

Of course. But if only I could take it—all.

EBEN

You can't. That's why you had no right to do it. Alison didn't.

ELSA

No. But she was Alison. She had God.

EBEN

Afraid God left her pretty lonely at times.

ELSA

Yes. That's why she wrote about Him as if He ought
to be more.

EBEN

How's Bill?

ELSA

Bill's all right. He misses the business, and his friends,
and the children. I can see him missing them.

EBEN

Lucky he has enough to live on.

ELSA

Yes. But that isn't enough.

EBEN

But you're happy?

ELSA

Happy, and unhappy.

EBEN

What did you run away like that for? Why didn't
you talk it over with me?

ELSA

You would have kept me from going.

EBEN

Of course I would!

ELSA

But I had to go, Eben. Don't you see? That was the way I loved him.

EBEN (*after watching her face*)

Wish I loved some one.

ELSA

I wish you did. (*Listening.*) They're coming.
[*She arranges the big chair.*

AGATHA (*as they come in*)

I'm no prisoner, am I? Why should I stay up in my room if I don't want to?
[*Her brother is steadying her arm; on her other arm swings a silk bag, closed by a draw-string. Both* EBEN *and* STANHOPE *help in seating her, more feeble than in the morning. As soon as she is seated she clutches for the bag, holding it.* ELSA *brings a footstool, which her aunt disregards.*

EBEN (*cheerfully*)

All right now?

AGATHA

If it's the last day I'll ever be here, then I want to *be* here.

EBEN

That's right, Aunt Agatha, and here we all are.

AGATHA

But tomorrow. We won't be here tomorrow.

ELSA

Then let's think about our being here today.

[*She sits on the footstool.* EBEN *throws more papers on the fire from the heap on the floor.*

AGATHA

Yes. Make it burn. (*Turning a little to see.*) Burn them. Burn them all. (*She clutches the bag.*) What are they?

EBEN

Old things we don't need any more.

AGATHA

Old things we don't need any more.
[STANHOPE, *who has been watching her, can bear it no longer, goes out.*

ELSA

You'll have your tea now, won't you, Aunt Agatha?

AGATHA (*after a moment of not coming from her own thought*)

What? No. No, I don't want it. (*She turns her head to the fire, taking the bag from her arm, holding it in her hands.*) Put on—old things we don't need any more.
[*After an anxious look at her,* EBEN *puts more papers on the fire.*

EBEN (*briskly*)

It's going to be fine for you up at Father's. That's going to be the most comfortable room you ever had.

AGATHA

If Elsa hadn't run away and left her father I wouldn't be turned out.

ELSA

I'm sorry, Aunt Agatha.

AGATHA (*quite differently*)

Little Elsa. (*With a low sob* ELSA *leans against her aunt.* EBEN *goes softly out. So they sit a moment,* AGATHA'S *hand on* ELSA'S *hair. But from this she goes into a curious, fixed state.*) Where is Alison?

ELSA

She isn't here. Though she seemed here, just a moment ago.

AGATHA

I have to take care of Alison.

ELSA

Yes. You always did.

AGATHA

I always did.

ELSA

Always.

AGATHA

But she—went away. How could I tell—what she wanted me to do? (*Pause.*) Who is looking at us?

ELSA

No one is looking at us. You and I are here alone.

AGATHA

You are Elsa?

ELSA

I am Elsa.

[*With trembling fingers* AGATHA *undoes the string of her bag and takes out a small leather portfolio. Looks fearfully around, looks at the fire. She tries to rise.*

ELSA

What is it, Aunt Agatha? I will do anything you want done.

AGATHA

You will—do anything—I want done?

ELSA

Why yes, Aunt Agatha. I will do anything in the world for you.

AGATHA

Elsa will do it. Elsa.

ELSA

Yes. Elsa will do it.

AGATHA

Then— (*She holds out the leather case, but withdraws it. Then suddenly gives it.*) Take it! For— Elsa.
[*She falls forward.*

ELSA (*frightened*)

Aunt Agatha! (*She leans her back in the chair, though not letting go the small portfolio* AGATHA *has given her. Becomes more frightened as she looks.*) Aunt Agatha! What is it? Speak to me! (*After another moment of growing fear she runs to the door.*) Father! Eben!
[EBEN *hurries in.*

EBEN

    What is it?

    [STANHOPE *enters.*

ELSA

    She—has she fainted?

STANHOPE (*bending over her*)

    Agatha! Agatha! (*On the other side* EBEN *takes one of her hands, he is feeling for her pulse.*)

    [EBEN *lays his head against her heart.*

EBEN (*looking up*)

    Why, Father, I don't—

    [*Her eyes are closed.* STANHOPE *lifts one of the lids, looking at the eye.*

ELSA

    Has she—fainted?

STANHOPE

    She has died.

    [ELSA, *who has not let go the leather case, presses it against her breast.*

EBEN

    It is better.

STANHOPE (*who is kneeling by her*)

    My sister! Agatha! Forgive me. (*Lifting his head, taking her two hands, looking into her face. Softly, as if putting her to sleep.*) Yes. Yes. Find Alison, dear. Find Alison.

CURTAIN

ACT THREE

ACT THREE

Scene: Alison's room. The door into the hall is rear, toward left; center, rear, a fireplace. Beyond this is a smaller door, as if opening into dressing-room or closet. At right, extending from rear, a single, four-poster bed. It has a light, flowered counter-pane. Right, front, a desk. There is a small stand near the head of the bed; between the bed and fireplace, a low easy chair. In the rear corner, left, an old bureau. In the middle of the room, though somewhat front, and left, an old-fashioned walnut table.

The curtains are white. The carpet is the color of gray-green moss.

A fire is burning, and the room is lighted by a lamp on the stand near the bed.

It nears the last hour of the century, a little after half past ten, evening of the same day.

The door opens slowly, and ELSA *comes in. She waits a moment by the door, as if to be asked to enter. Then goes to the fire, holding out her hands. She looks at the clock, on the fireplace mantel. Winds, sets it, consulting her watch. Turns, standing uncertainly a moment. Goes slowly to the desk. Looks at a picture in a gold, oval frame, which hangs over the desk. She opens a drawer and takes out the portfolio her Aunt Agatha gave her. Stands there holding it. She is about to sit at the desk, but steps back from it, as if it is not for her to sit there. Goes to the table; putting the portfolio there,*

111

*she goes to the mantel, where are two silver candle sticks.
Lights them, and takes them to the table. She sits down,
and after holding the portfolio a moment, spreads it out
as if to open the pockets. (It is one of those flexible cases
which doubles over.) She is opening one side when there
is a knock at the door.*

ELSA (*putting the portfolio on the table*)
   Come in.

ANN
   May I? Just a moment?

ELSA
   Of course, Ann.

ANN (*looking around*)
   Alison's room. As if—as if she might be going to bed
   here.

ELSA
   I have been thinking of that. Father said I might
   sleep here tonight. Eben asked him. (*Pause.*) Won't
   you sit down, dear?
   [ANN *comes to the table, sits.*

ANN
   I feel I shouldn't be here. I know you are tired, and
   want to be alone in this room. I'll only stay a minute.

ELSA
   I'm glad you came.

ANN (*impulsively, yet timid*)
   I was so glad to see you, Elsa, when you came.

ELSA (*grateful*)

>You were?

ANN

>Oh, yes. So were Eben and Ted.

ELSA

>But Father—

ANN

>He can't help it, can he?

ELSA

>No. Of course not. But—I did so want to come. (*Shaking her head.*) It wasn't that I wanted to. I had to.

ANN

>You had to be here once more.

ELSA.

>The last time.

ANN

>It's hard.

ELSA

>I used to come to this room when things went wrong. "Come to Alison, dear," she'd say. Or "Whatever is wrong, Alison will make it right." (*Pause.*) If only she could!

ANN

>Perhaps she can.

ELSA

I fear not. I have gone—out of her world.

ANN

I'm not sure she would think so.

ELSA

Perhaps not. For—really—you couldn't go out of
her world. She was everywhere. She knew.

ANN

I didn't know her but—it does seem that way. What
did I say? I didn't know her? But I do know her.
Her poems let me know her. And now—tonight—I
know her better than before. (ELSA *only waits in
inquiry.*) Elsa! Can you fall in love, all at once, with
somebody you don't know?

ELSA (*looking at the picture over the desk*)

Ask Alison.

ANN (*following her look*)

Is that—his picture?

ELSA

Yes. It was always there—as long as I can remember.

ANN (*going to it*)

How strange the clothes look.

ELSA

Ours will look strange too, in thirty years.

ANN

Why I suppose they will. They seem so right now.

ELSA

Nothing stays right—forever.

ANN (*turning to her*)

Love does.

ELSA (*with a little laugh*)

Love doesn't have to clothe itself.

ANN (*coming back to her*)

Then you think it really can be love, though it happens—all at once?

ELSA

It has happened too often for me to say it can't be true. Though it wasn't that way with me.

ANN

You and Bill had known each other a long time.

ELSA

Since I had braids down my back. And he never used to be—different from any one else. And then—all of a sudden— We had been dancing; we stopped by the door. We just looked at each other—stared, rather, and he said— "Why, Elsa!" We stood there, and then he said, "It is Elsa." And we went out to the verandah, and everything was different, because he was Bill and I was Elsa.

ANN

So it did happen suddenly, after all.

ELSA

And everything we had together in the past—when we used to slide down hill together—was there, alive, giving us a past we hadn't known we were making for ourselves.

ANN

I think it is a miracle, don't you?

ELSA

Yes, I think it is a miracle. Though it's a miracle you have to pay for, sometimes.

ANN

Always, perhaps.

ELSA

I don't know. Often it goes happily. It's nice that you don't have to hurt any one.

ANN

But I do, I fear. He was almost engaged. Not quite. Elsa! His name is Richard.

ELSA

Richard is a nice name.

ANN

I shall never call him Dick. Richard I think is better for him. (ELSA *nods gravely*.) And to think it was Alison brought us together! That is like a blessing, don't you think?

ELSA

I do think so.

ANN

It was wonderful—down by the river, thinking of all that happened in this century that is going, of all that

will happen in the century that is right here now, for
us. (*She is lost in this a moment.*) Perhaps it seems
cruel we should be sitting here talking of love, with
poor Miss Agatha dead just across the hall.

ELSA

It is the way it is.

ANN

And it is strange: She was so good, but she does seem
dead, and Alison, dead eighteen years, is here. (ELSA's
hand moves, rests on the portfolio.) Elsa, I came to
ask you something, and I'm sorry it seems I came for
a purpose—a favor, because I stayed down here
hoping to have a talk with you, but—

ELSA

What is it, dear? I will do it, if I can.

ANN

You see Richard has to think of—the story. In spite
of— (*An excited little laugh.*) everything else, he has
to think of the paper. And it's more of a story now,
Alison's sister dying just as she is leaving the house
where she and Alison lived together.

ELSA

Yes, I suppose it is more of a story.

ANN

And he needs a picture of Miss Agatha.

ELSA

You would have to ask Father about that.

ANN

How can I? He's with *her.*

ELSA

But you see I haven't—the right. Ask Eben.

ANN

Eben is so strange. He's down in the library, reading
the books, and he doesn't look up when you come in,
or hear you when you speak. So I thought—I can't
talk to the others, but I believe I could talk to Elsa.
I always wanted to talk to you. I always had—sounds
foolish—a sort of case on you. All the younger girls
did. Elsa Stanhope—they'd say. As if you were what
they wanted to be.

ELSA

Oh—Ann.

ANN

It seemed you had everything. Beautiful—a Stanhope
—so nice to everyone, yet always holding yourself
a little apart. We used to think of you as a princess.

ELSA (*after looking at her in silence a moment*)

And then I—went back on you, didn't I?

ANN

It was—a shock. But we thought you were brave.

ELSA

I wasn't brave. I was trapped. I didn't think it was
right—but I couldn't help myself. And Bill. When
you love, you want to give your man—everything in
the world.

ANN

Everything.

ELSA

But in giving to him, I took so much away from him.

ANN (*for a moment not intruding on all* ELSA *is feeling*)
But you love each other—as much as ever.

ELSA

Our love is a flame—burning fiercely—in sorrow.
(*Coming from this.*) I wish I could say yes about the
picture, Ann. There is one here.
[*She goes to the desk, takes a picture from the drawer.*
ANN *goes to her, they look at it.*

ANN

Oh, it's a *dear*. She was much younger then.

ELSA

Taken years ago, before Alison died.

ANN

When she was Agatha, while Alison was Alison.

ELSA (*nodding*)
It never would have occurred to her to have one taken
afterwards. She thought she was just for Alison.

ANN

She worshipped her.

ELSA

And guarded her, her whole life through. I'd really
like to give it to you, for her own sake. Aunt Agatha,
who lived always in this house, now wanted, for a
moment, by the world. She was so good. And she will

pass—so soon. I'd like to talk to your Richard, and tell him how good she was.

ANN

Oh, *would* you, Elsa?

ELSA

But I haven't the right to speak for the family. (*A knock.*) Come in. (EBEN *enters.*) I thought you'd come, Eben.

EBEN (*with an emotional, rather reckless laugh*)

See the New Year in.

ANN (*softly*)

Will you ask him?

ELSA

Eben, Ann wants this picture of Aunt Agatha, to give to her reporter.

EBEN

She's in love with him.

ELSA (*laughing*)

It certainly looks that way.

EBEN

Are you going to marry him, Ann?

ANN

What else can I do?
[*They all laugh a little.*

EBEN

And go away and leave Father?

ANN

What else can I do?

EBEN

Poor Father. We all want to go away and leave him.

ELSA

You won't, Eben.

EBEN

What else can I do—but stay? (*Pause.*) I don't know about the picture. You'd have to ask Father.

ANN

He's with his sister.

EBEN

And she too—went away and left him. (*He holds out his hand for the picture.*) Remember her that way, Elsa?

ELSA

I remember.

EBEN

And then she got old, and strange. Yes—yes, take it. Let her have—one moment of youth.

ANN

Oh, *thank* you, Eben. You know, I think you are right.

EBEN

Oh, yes, you would think so. Easy to call it right, when it's what you want to do. Don't mind me, Ann. Just talking to myself.

ANN

I do thank you. And I do think you are right.

EBEN

Well, that's good.

ANN

Good night.

ELSA

Good night, Ann. Many happy new years.

ANN

Thank you. And to you.

ELSA

Thank you.
[ANN *goes.*

EBEN

You've no idea how Father will miss her. Seems a pretty sudden decision. You see, I don't *get* it. You are yourself for years and years, and then some other self, you don't know at all, is more to you than anything else. It's like building up something—only to throw it down.

ELSA

And then it all means something.

EBEN

Does it? Poor Father. It isn't only that Ann is so helpful to him, but he has a particular feeling about her. I wonder how long Mother and Father were happy together?

ELSA

I don't remember them as happy.

EBEN

I suspect he gave up a lot. I almost know it—felt I shouldn't know. And what's he left with? I don't see Ted comforting any one's old age.

ELSA

But I think he may. He's so much like every one else.

EBEN

Dreary picture of the world.

ELSA

Though you are Father's greatest comfort, Eben.

EBEN

Then I can only say again—poor Father.

ELSA

What's the matter, Eben?

EBEN (*considering talking to her, putting it off*)

It's a good thing you were here—when it happened. Father would have sent for you.

ELSA

Yes, I think he would want me to be here—now.

EBEN (*standing by the fire*)

The clock is going.

ELSA

I wanted it to tell—the last hour.

EBEN

As it told the hours for Alison. Don't you suppose
they seemed pretty long at times?

ELSA

Here—she should be sitting.
[*Her hand on the chair by the fire.*

EBEN

Unless— (*He goes over to the desk, puts his hand on
that chair.*) Here. (*Standing back, as if looking at
ALISON.*) She is sitting here with her papers—with her
thoughts, and the words for her thoughts. She is wearing a white dress. The full skirt spreads out from the
chair. The sleeves too are full, and her small hands
hover over what she has. Her eyes— Heavens! Have I
forgotten them?

ELSA

They are clear—like golden wine.

EBEN

Her brown hair is parted in the middle, and held
loosely at the neck. She is looking straight ahead, as
if into something. But she is really waiting for the
right word to come. They came, you can tell that.
They were willing visitors. She didn't have to go out
and pull them in. There is a knock at the door. It's
me. I am crying. She makes a funny little face. She
says— Tell Allison. I tell her Jimmy Miles has knocked
over my mud house. She says— You can build a fort,
and put him in it. She tells me the story of the bumble bee that got drunk on larkspur and set out to see

how drunk you could get in heaven. And what became of her thoughts—the thought I interrupted?

ELSA

Oh it waited for her, and the bumble bee came into it.

EBEN

And that was his heaven.

ELSA

Why not? (*They are both brighter.*) Then another knock. No, a pounding with fists—Alison—Alison. Little Elsa! Aunt Agatha won't give me a cookie, because I pulled the cat's tail. She tells me Aunt Agatha can't help being like that, and that the cat would agree with her. And she says—what if I had pulled the tail off, and we laugh; and she writes me a little poem, about a cookie that had no tail. She gives me candy, and stands at the door so Aunt Agatha can't get in, but God, she says, could come down the chimney. (*They both laugh.* ELSA *goes over to the table, takes up the portfolio she was about to open when* ANN *came in. Slowly.*) I don't know what is in this.

EBEN

Where did you get it? (*A knock at the door.*) Come in. [STANHOPE *opens the door. Stands there a moment before closing it. Continues to stand near the door.*

STANHOPE (*as if to himself*)

I wish I could talk with Alison.

EBEN

Come into her room, Father. Do sit down. You look tired out.

[STANHOPE *sits in the chair near the fire;* EBEN *sits by the desk,* ELSA *at the table. A long pause.*

STANHOPE

The funeral must be down here.

EBEN

Yes. I think so too.

STANHOPE

It means a good deal of work, but I won't take her out of her house. Not into another—house.

EBEN

Things can be straightened around enough—for that.

STANHOPE

How badly we did it.

EBEN

We did the best we could.

STANHOPE

Poor consolation. (*After a moment he turns directly to* ELSA.) You were alone with your aunt when she died.

ELSA

Yes, Father.

STANHOPE

What did she say?

ELSA

The last thing?

STANHOPE

Yes.

ELSA

She said— For Elsa.

STANHOPE

What did she mean?

ELSA

I don't know—yet.

STANHOPE

You were holding a little leather case that Alison used.

ELSA

Yes.

STANHOPE

Where did you get it?

ELSA

Aunt Agatha gave it to me.

STANHOPE

And it was then she said—

ELSA

For Elsa.

STANHOPE

What is in it?

ELSA

I don't know yet.

STANHOPE

Open it and see.
[ELSA *hesitates, looks to* EBEN.

EBEN

But it's Elsa's, isn't it, Father, if Aunt Agatha gave
it to her?

STANHOPE

It belongs to the family. Agatha didn't know what
she was doing. Where is it? (ELSA *takes it from the
table.*) Open it.
[*There is a knock at the door.*

ELSA (*after waiting for one of the others to speak*)
Come.
[JENNIE *enters.*

JENNIE (*who seems confused at seeing the two men*)
Oh, I thought it was just Miss Elsa.
[*Stands uncertainly, troubled.*

ELSA

What is it, Jennie?

JENNIE

Never mind—now.
[*But stands there.*

EBEN

Did you want something?

JENNIE

Yes.

EBEN

Well, what?

JENNIE

She told me to.

STANHOPE

Who?

JENNIE

Her. Miss Agatha.

EBEN

Told you what?
[JENNIE *goes to the desk, starts to open a drawer, turns to* STANHOPE.

JENNIE

Excuse me, but I gave my promise. (*Looks.*) It's gone! Where is it?

STANHOPE

Where is what, Jennie?

JENNIE

Give it to me! I gave my promise.

EBEN

You'll have to tell us a little more, Jennie. We don't know what you are talking about.

JENNIE

All these last days—after she got the idea—and couldn't—it was always the same— "Make the fire,

Jennie. Put on more wood—make it burn"—and she'd
sit by it—and couldn't.

STANHOPE

Couldn't *what?*

JENNIE

Do it herself. So she'd tell me—and each time I'd
promise.

EBEN

What did you promise, Jennie?

JENNIE (*a little impatiently*)

To do it for her, if she died before—— Where *is* it? It
isn't here—— (*Looking again in the drawer, then in the
pigeon holes.*) or here.

[STANHOPE, *rising, takes the portfolio from* ELSA,
who almost resists, and rises.

ELSA

No! It is mine!

STANHOPE (*to* JENNIE)

Is this what you are looking for?

JENNIE

That's it! Oh, give it to me! Please give it to me—
so's I can carry out my promise. I could never draw
another easy breath if——

STANHOPE

What did Miss Agatha say about it?

JENNIE

Nothing. Only she'd try—and couldn't. Get it—then

bring it back here. Give it to me—so I can carry out my promise!

EBEN

Just what did you promise, Jennie?

STANHOPE (*as* JENNIE *does not reply*)

Answer, please. What did you promise?

JENNIE

I promised to burn it.

ELSA (*low*)

Oh, no!

STANHOPE

My sister must have changed her mind. She gave this to Miss Elsa.

JENNIE

Then she wanted *you* to—

STANHOPE

Is that it? Did she ask you to burn it?

ELSA (*shaking her head*)

She held it out to me—started to take it back—then gave it, said— For Elsa, and died.

EBEN

That certainly makes it Elsa's.

JENNIE

I was to do it, the very night she—couldn't. I won't sleep a wink tonight unless—

STANHOPE

Yes you will sleep, Jennie. This is a family matter. You may rest assured I will see that the right thing is done.

JENNIE (*after standing there helplessly*)

Well, I can't help it, can I?

STANHOPE

No, it is out of your hands now.

EBEN

It's after half past ten, Jennie. Better get some rest. You'll have a hard day tomorrow.

JENNIE (*looking from him to his father*)

I looked after her—thirty years. And I did for Miss Alison, when we had Miss Alison. What am I going to do—now?

STANHOPE

Of course you know we will always look after you, Jennie.

JENNIE

But who—who will I look after?

STANHOPE

Oh you'll have to look after me.

JENNIE

You have so many.

STANHOPE

Have I?

JENNIE (*moving to the door*)

Well— (*Turning back.*) That was why she tried to burn the house—burn it all together, because she couldn't burn it alone. You can tell by that—how much she wanted to do it.

EBEN

And how impossible it was to do it.

JENNIE

But I could do it. I wouldn't even look at it. I promised not to. I would put it in the kitchen stove, put down the lid, and wait. Then I was to stir the ashes, to make sure.

STANHOPE

Good night, Jennie. I promise you again, the right thing will be done.

JENNIE

Good night.

EBEN

Good night, Jennie. (*She goes.*) Poor old thing. Remember all the good things she used to make for us, Elsa?

ELSA

Cookies with nuts in them.

EBEN

Doughnuts sprinkled with sugar. (*Looking at his father, who has returned to his chair, spread the portfolio on his lap, and is about to open it.*) If you will forgive me, Father, you're awfully tired now, I

think you would feel better about it—afterwards, to
let Elsa open the package Aunt Agatha gave her and
see whether it is for all of us.

[STANHOPE, *after considering, holds the portfolio out
to* ELSA.

ELSA (*taking it*)

Thank you, Father. (*She sits at the table. Uncertainly, to* EBEN.) Shall I open it now?

EBEN

If you will. Why not?

ELSA (*she puts the case on the table, spreads it out.
Nervously, to* EBEN)

Perhaps you had better do it.

EBEN

No, open it.
[*She unfastens one side, takes out a slender package
of old papers, tied with a thread.*

EBEN

Why that's like—

ELSA (*feeling it*)

It's the paper Alison used for—for her— (*Taking
out others.*) All tied—that same way.

EBEN

The way *she* tied them. (*After a pause.*) Undo one
of them.
[ELSA *tries to untie the knot, has trouble with it.*

STANHOPE

Break that thread!
[ELSA *does so, and unfolds a long sheet of old paper.*

EBEN

Alison's writing!

STANHOPE (*sharply*)

What are they?

ELSA (*reading*)

Why—they are—they are—

EBEN (*reading over her shoulder*)

Are they—*poems?* (*He takes one from another pack-age, then opens still another. As if he cannot believe it.*) All of them. (*He takes a package to his father.*) They are Alison's. They are poems. Poems we never saw. (STANHOPE *examines one.*) They are her poems, aren't they?

STANHOPE (*slowly*)

No one else—that ever lived—would say it just that way.

EBEN

But Father—had you known about them?

STANHOPE

I did not know they existed.

EBEN

But *why?* (*Showing one he is himself reading.*) See? She never wrote a thing—more Alison.

STANHOPE (*reading it*)

Alison—at her best.

EBEN

Then I just can't understand it! Where have they been? *Why?* My *God*—was it *this* Aunt Agatha thought she must burn?

STANHOPE

I don't understand it.

ELSA (*who has been reading*)

O-h, I think I do.

EBEN (*about to speak to her, but she is deeply absorbed, turns again to his father*)

But Father—this is of immense importance! Look at them! Why I believe it's almost as many as we published! Coming now—when she has her place—you know all they say about her—now—so much later—all of these— But *why?*

ELSA

Alison!

[*Her head goes down among the papers. The two men look at her. There is a tap at the door.* TED *comes in, wearing outdoor things. At the interruption,* ELSA *raises her head, and while he is there goes on reading.*

TED (*going to his father*)

I'm sorry, Father—about Aunt Agatha. Know how you feel. I'm— (*Feels awkward.*) Gee, I had an awful time getting here. Awfully sorry not to have been here before. You see I was at the Martin's, and Louise didn't know that, so I didn't get the word till I got to the dance. (*Turning to* EBEN, *as his father does not seem to hear him.*) Started on my bike. Gee, those ruts, in the dark. Had to walk from the Swartz'. Thought I was never going to get here.

EBEN (*still dazed*)

You were good to try so hard. Glad you're here.

TED

Must have happened just after I left.

EBEN

Yes. At four-fifteen.

TED

Louise'll be down first thing in the morning. She's awfully sorry she can't be here tonight.

EBEN

It's just as— That's all right.

TED (*looking at his father*)

Well, gee I'm— (*Looking from one to the other.*) Course I know how you all feel. (*As no one speaks he stoops to pick up a paper* ELSA *has brushed to the floor.*) That's Alison's writing. (*Reading.*) It's a poem. Guess I don't know that one. (*Looking up at* EBEN.) Why I thought the manuscripts were all at the State Historical Society. (*Putting it on the table he takes up another.*) Don't seem to remember this one, either. (*Turning over others.*) Say! Where did these come from?

EBEN

We have just found them.

TED

Found them? Where were they?

EBEN

Aunt Agatha had them.

TED

And never— For Pete's sake! (*Suddenly excited.*)
Why say, that's important, isn't it?

EBEN (*nodding, speaking low*)

Father's pretty—done up by this, after—everything
else. Just leave him here with us now. You can look at
those tomorrow.

TED (*looking at his father*)

Well—all right. (*Going reluctantly to the door.*) But
gee, what did Aunt Agatha want to hide them for?

EBEN

We don't know. She must have thought it was the
right thing to do.

TED

Don't see how she figured *that* out.

EBEN

We can talk about it tomorrow. (*As* TED *is closing the
door.*) Don't say anything about it!

STANHOPE (*looking up*)

No!

TED

Gee!

[*He goes.*

EBEN (*regarding his father*)

Don't you think we'd better put them away for tonight! They're too important for now. Hadn't you
better get to bed, Father?

STANHOPE (*to* ELSA)

Why did you say her name like that?

ELSA

Because she was telling me her story. It's here—the
story she never told. She has written it, as it was never
written before. The love that never died—loneliness
that never died—anguish and beauty of her love! I
said her name because she was with me.

[STANHOPE *holds out his hand.*

EBEN

Not tonight.

[*But as* STANHOPE *continues to hold out his hand*
EBEN *gives him the poems* ELSA *had been reading. He
and* ELSA *sit by the table, bending over others.*

EBEN (*low, and in beautiful excitement*)

Why that bird sang—thirty years ago, and sings
now.

ELSA

But *her—her.*

EBEN

But the way she kept it all in life. I can see that flower
bend, and smell it.

STANHOPE (*simply*)

 I can not bear it.

EBEN (*going to him and trying to take the poems*)

 Don't read them tonight, Father.

 [*But* STANHOPE *keeps them, and takes up another.*
 EBEN *goes back to the table.*

ELSA (*speaking to what she reads*)

 Yes. I know.

 [*The clock strikes eleven. A dimming of the lights indi-
 cates the passing of time. A moment's darkness. When
 the lights rise* ELSA *still sits at the table, as if she has
 had a great experience, as if she has come to know
 something, and has the courage to know it.* EBEN *has
 moved, and is standing by the fire.* STANHOPE *sits as he
 was, bowed over the papers still in his lap. After a
 moment the clock strikes the half hour.*

EBEN (*slowly, as if trying to realize it*)

 And all of that—went on in this room.

STANHOPE

 If I had known it was, as much as this—I would not
 have asked her to stay.

ELSA

 You did ask her to stay?

STANHOPE

 In this room I asked her to stay. He was below. He
 had come for her.

EBEN

 I never really knew the story.

STANHOPE

She had gone East, with Father, to Cambridge, Thirtieth reunion of Father's class. She met him there. He was a teacher of English, at Harvard. At once they seemed to recognize each other. He was for her. She was for him. That was—without question. But he was married. He had children. They parted. But— they were one. I know that now.

EBEN

And it was after that—all those years after that— she played with us, Elsa—loved her flowers—comforted us and gave us the little presents.

ELSA

It was death for her. But she made it—life eternal.

EBEN (*so moved it is hard to speak*)

Never mind, Alison. We have found you.

ELSA

You will never be alone again.
[*A knock.* TED *comes in.*

TED

I want to read some of the poems. (*As no one speaks.*) Well, gee, I'm of the family too, ain't I? If you don't want me here I'll take some of them down to the library.

STANHOPE

They will not be taken from this room.

TED

All right, then I'll read them here.

EBEN

Not now.

TED

They're mine as much as yours, aren't they?

STANHOPE

I will protect my sister. I will do—what Agatha could not do.

EBEN (*sharply*)

What do you mean?

STANHOPE

They were for her alone. She does not have to show her heart to the world.

ELSA

Father! You don't mean— Tell us you don't mean—!

STANHOPE

I mean that I am going to burn them in her own fire-place—before her century goes.

EBEN

Father!

ELSA (*gathering up the papers*)

No!

TED

And *I* say— No! They're ours too, aren't they?

STANHOPE

I shall protect my sister, if it's the last thing I do on earth.

EBEN

She isn't just your sister, Father.

TED

I should say not! She's Alison.

STANHOPE

And she could help get you through Harvard, couldn't she? What luck! Send a wire to your teacher! Get your grade!

EBEN

Steady now, Father. There's been too much today. No decisions can be made tonight.

STANHOPE

If they're not made tonight, they will never be made. [*He rises.*

TED

Now here I object. Here *I* step in. *I'll* protect Alison. I'm younger than you are. I can do it better.

EBEN

Leave it to us, Ted.

TED

I'll not leave it to anybody! I am Alison Stanhope's nephew and I will not have her poems burned. Understand?

STANHOPE

Leave the room!

TED

Oh no, Father, you can't go on doing that. I'll be alive

when the rest of you are dead. Then *I'm* the one to look after them.

[*With a swift movement he puts some of the papers in his pocket, reaches for others.*

STANHOPE (*springing at him*)

Drop them! Drop them or I'll kill you!

EBEN

Father!

[STANHOPE, *overcome by what he has said, steps back.* EBEN *comes between him and* TED.

EBEN (*to* TED)

I agree with you. I want what you want. The poems must be kept. But the way you go at it would make anybody want to knock you down.

TED

All right. Knock me down. Try it.

EBEN

Shut up. Use some judgment. Can't you see Father's worn out?

TED

I'm not.

ELSA

Oh, Ted! *Please.* Here in Alison's room, Aunt Agatha dead across the hall, must we *quarrel?*

EBEN

Go away, Ted. Elsa and I will talk to Father. You have no sense.

TED

I've sense enough to know the value of things.

STANHOPE

They're almost as valuable as rubber tires, aren't they?

ELSA

Please go away now. We promise you it will be all right.

STANHOPE

I promise you my sister's intimate papers are not going into your vulgar world.
[TED *snatches for more of them.* EBEN *seizes him.*

EBEN

I'm a match for you yet! Don't be so damned sure you'll be alive when I am dead! And what if you are? You're alive now, and what of it? What do you amount to?

TED

I'll show you what I amount to!
[*He tries to break from* EBEN's *grip.* ELSA *comes behind them, one hand on* EBEN's *shoulder, the other on* TED's.

ELSA (*quietly*)

Oh this isn't the way we act in our family. (EBEN *steps back.*) Come, Ted dear. I ask you to go. And leave them to me. I know their value—as no one else knows.

TED (*looking hard at her*)

    All right, Elsa. I trust them to you. Not Eben. Not Father. I leave them with Elsa.
    [*He goes.*

STANHOPE

    He has some of them.

EBEN

    It's all right, Father. Ted is really all right.
    [*With a groan,* STANHOPE *sinks to his chair, burying his face in his hands.*

EBEN (*looking anxiously at him*)

    Let's have a little sherry—for the New Year.
    [*He goes.*

ELSA (*after he has raised his head*)

    Ted's exasperating, but of course you didn't mean it, Father. You couldn't mean it. It's Alison's heart. You wouldn't keep that from—living in the world she loved.

STANHOPE

    Living in *your* world? Linked with—*you?* As if—

ELSA

    Don't say it, Father. She wouldn't. She would understand. Alison knew. And do you know, I think she would be glad?

STANHOPE

    Glad you ran away with a married man—living in shame and leaving misery behind you?

ELSA

> Glad I have my love. In spite of—all the rest. Know-
> ing what it is to be alone, I think she would be glad I
> am not alone. What could I do—alone? How could I
> —Elsa—find victory in defeat? For you see, I am not
> enough. She would know that. She would be tolerant.
> She would be gentle—oh, so gentle. If she were here
> now—in her own room—she would say— Happy? Are
> you happy? Be happy, little Elsa, she would say.
> [EBEN *returns with the tray of bottle and glasses.*

EBEN (*pouring the wine, trying to speak naturally*)

> Well, it's a trial, having Ted in the family. It's a
> chore. Though do you know—I rather liked him.
> (*Giving his father the glass.*) Keep in mind, Father,
> how Alison loved the kids of the family.

ELSA (*holding her drink before the candle*)

> That was the color of her eyes.

EBEN (*raising his glass*)

> To Alison's love of youth!

ELSA (*as if speaking to her*)

> Alison.

STANHOPE

> To my sister, who loved to the uttermost, and denied,
> because it was right.
> [*After drinking a little,* EBEN *begins arranging the
> papers, which are in confusion.*

STANHOPE

> Gather them up. Put them as they were.
> [ELSA *helps him.*

EBEN (*who has paused to read, and smiles at something he sees*)

No question about it. They were too big for just us. They are for the world.

STANHOPE

In justification of myself—I am so tired of justifying myself that I wish—I wish I were with Agatha—but I ask you, did she give them to the world?

EBEN

She didn't give the others to the world, either. She was too timid of the world. She just left them, and we did the right thing, as in her heart she knew we would.

STANHOPE

These were not left with the others. Where were they left? What did she tell Agatha?

EBEN

We don't know their story, and now we won't know it, for Aunt Agatha can't tell us. But we know they are here, alive, and we know we will do the right thing.

STANHOPE

Yes. We will do the right thing.
[*He goes to the fire, stirs it. There is a knock.* ANN *comes in followed by* TED *and* KNOWLES.

ANN

I'm sorry to come in here now. But I couldn't help it.
[STANHOPE, *as if unable to bear the thought there is more to meet, sinks to his chair.*

KNOWLES

And I'm sorry. You've been so good to me, and I've been such a nuisance on a hard day. But when I realized I was the only one from the outside who knew, I—I had to come. It was my duty, sir.

EBEN (*to* TED)

So you told.

TED

You think you can keep them to yourself. Ask *anybody. Anybody.*

ANN (*going to* STANHOPE, *and sitting in a low seat beside him*)

You were so good to me, always. I feel as if you were my father, though I know you're not, really. You were so good to Mother. (*Low.*) You loved her. And she loved you. Through years. And you denied your love, because of me, and Eben, and Elsa, and Ted. Well, here we all are—the children—Eben, Elsa, Ted, and Ann. Can't you let us, now when you are old, and sad, tell you what to do—for us? Won't you let Alison's words pass on—as a gift to all love—let them *be* here—when you are not here?

STANHOPE

Ann! Don't!

ANN

I must. It is too important. I know that now. I know tonight, better than I would have known last night.

STANHOPE (*his hands falling at his sides*)

I cannot make it plain to you, but she was of an age

when people did not tell their love. She held it deep in her heart. Then can I let her tell it now, to serve you?

ANN

Yes.

STANHOPE (*turning his face away*)

I cannot bear—your youth.

ANN

Will you promise me to leave it to Elsa?

STANHOPE

Elsa! Why should I leave it to Elsa?

ANN

To a woman. Because Alison said it—for women.

STANHOPE

Alison was not like Elsa. Alison stayed.

ELSA

Then let her speak for Elsa, and Mother, and me. Let her have *that* from it. For her own sake—let her have that from it!

EBEN

Yes. I think Father will leave it to Elsa. And now the rest of you, please go.

ANN (*making a move to go, but turning back*)

I don't want you to do it, because I have a great love for you, and I don't want you, when dying, to feel, I am guilty, I took life.

[*She goes out.* TED *starts after her, but as* KNOWLES *steps forward* TED *stands in the doorway.*

KNOWLES (*very simply, but as if the words have a great mission*)

> "She lays her beams in music,
>   In music every one,
> To the cadence of the whirling world
>   Which dances round the sun.
>
> That so they shall not be displaced
>   By lapses or by wars,
> But for the love of happy souls
>   Outlive the newest stars."

[*Stands silent, motionless a moment, goes.*

EBEN (*after a little time*)

Enough for one night, isn't it? One thing we know. Aunt Agatha left the poems to Elsa. For the time being then, they are with Elsa. After—after the funeral, we can decide just what to do. (*Pause.*) Good night, Father. (*No reply.*) Good night, Elsa.

ELSA

Eben! Don't leave me.

EBEN (*with a nod, as to say, it is better*)

Yes.
[*He goes.*

ELSA (*after a pause, low*)

I didn't know, Father, that you had gone through it too.

STANHOPE

Did you think I was happy with your mother?

ELSA

No.

STANHOPE

And why did I stay? For you, and your brothers.
Mostly, for you.

ELSA

And then I—

STANHOPE

Then you—made it all nothing.

ELSA

I must seem—all wrong to you, Father.

STANHOPE

You are wrong. You did not think of others, and that
is wrong. And don't you know what this would say?
It would say— They are like that. They were always
like that. Louise is right there.

ELSA

Oh, Father—Louise! Our little town! Is that the thing
to think of—when Alison has spoken?

STANHOPE

Our little town is our lives. It's Eben's children.

ELSA

And what will be wrong with Eben's children—that
they can't love, and understand? You do. Eben does.
Have faith, Father. Trust them to understand.

STANHOPE (*as a cry from deep*)

Oh, Elsa! Why did you go away—and besmirch the name Alison held high? (*A sound from* ELSA, *a sobbing under her breath.*) And now—because of you—

ELSA

Don't, Father. Don't say it. She wouldn't. You ought to hurt me—some. But don't be that cruel, to make me feel—because of me—she can't go on. I loved, Father. I loved so much that—

STANHOPE

It is possible to love so much you can live without your love.

ELSA

I suppose it is possible, if you are a very great soul, or have a very stern sense of duty. But do you know, Father, I feel Alison wrote those poems for me.

STANHOPE

I feel she wrote them for me.

ELSA

And there will be those in the future to say, She wrote them for me.

STANHOPE

I feel—something right, something that all the time had to be, in you and me, here alone in her room, giving back to her century what she felt and did not say.

ELSA

But she did say.

STANHOPE

For herself alone.

ELSA

How can you know that? And even so— What has been brought into life cannot be taken from life.
[STANHOPE *goes to the fire, puts on more wood.*

STANHOPE

I never thought you and I would do another thing together. But she did love you. Then shield her. Join with me. What went on in this room—let it end in this room. It is right.
[*He goes to the table and takes the portfolio.*

ELSA (*standing between him and the fire*)

Father! The birds that sang thirty years ago. (*Her hands go out, as birds.*) The flower that bent in the wind.
[*She bends, as in the wind. The clock gives the first stroke of twelve. He stands motionless, listening.*

ELSA (*choked with tears*)

Happy New Year, Father.

STANHOPE (*mechanically*)

Happy— (*From a distance are bells in the village, whistles, a few shots. He looks around the room, hearing the bells. He looks long at* ELSA.) It isn't—what you said. Or even, what Ann said. But her. It goes. It is going. It is gone. She loved to make her little gifts. If she can make one more, from her century to yours, then she isn't gone. Anything else is—too lonely. (*He holds the poems out to her.*) For Elsa— From Alison.

ELSA (*taking them*)

Father! My father!

STANHOPE (*his arms around her*)

Little Elsa.

[*He holds her close while distant bells ring in the century.*

CURTAIN